puppet talk

Ideas for making puppets - and their use in the development
of language skills with children from four to nine years

Lilian Coppock

Line drawings by Glenn Goodwin

First Published in 1997 by
BELAIR PUBLICATIONS LIMITED
P.O. Box 12, Twickenham, England, TW1 2QL

© 1997 Lilian Coppock
Series Editor Robyn Gordon
Designed by Lynn Hooker
Photography by Kelvin Freeman
Printed in Hong Kong through World Print Ltd
ISBN 0 947882 59 6

Belair
Publications

Acknowledgements

The author and publishers would like to thank the children of Orleans Infant School, Richmond-upon-Thames, for their boundless enthusiasm for making puppets, and their ideas and suggestions.

The author would also like to thank Ken Dalston of Kendal Entertainments, Englefield Green, for his encouragement and inspiration, and the use of his original ideas on pages 5 and 29.

Up the tall white candlestick
Went little Mousie Brown
Right to the top, and he couldn't get down
So he called for his Grandma
'Grandma, Grandma'
But Grandma was in town
So he curled himself into a ball
And rolled himself right down.

Anon.

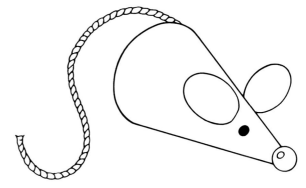

See 'Rhymes with Prepositions' on page 13

See Putting on a Performance on page 60

Where full reference to recommended books is not given in text, details are listed on page 71.

Contents

Introduction

For hundreds of years, all around the world, puppet shows have entertained adults and children, telling stories and transmitting messages and information - in spiritual and secular contexts. A puppet possesses a special magic, needing a human to give it life, and transporting the audience into an imaginative world where anything might happen. Objects may have a life of their own on the stage - a broom might sweep by itself and sing a song, or a ball may talk and play hide and seek with its owner.

Through playing with puppets, children can escape from their everyday world. Inhibitions are lost while hiding behind the mask of a puppet; emotions can be revealed, and sensitive areas can be explored in a safe context, without the risk of embarrassment. A puppet is not just an extension of the arm, but of the self.

Making puppets helps to develop knowledge and skills in many curricular areas, and has far more to offer than just a one-off craft activity. Many kinds of project work can be enhanced by the inclusion of puppet-making. It provides an opportunity for introducing multicultural work - traditions, folklore, history and costume. Children will need to draw on skills from maths when estimating, measuring and working in three dimensions. Learning the uses and properties of different materials, such as wood, papers, fabrics, plastics and feathers, will link with knowledge in science.

Making puppets helps to develop fine motor skills, and provides a stimulating purpose for design, technology and art: children will investigate how things work, develop their own ideas, learn how to use tools, fixings, fastenings and materials, and experiment with different finishes.

Puppets inspire the imagination and motivate creative thinking, providing an exciting opening for drama and creative writing. Stories, music and poetry can be brought to life. In addition, puppetry allows children of diverse abilities to work together, with a unique opportunity to participate, co-operate and share experiences.

Above all, puppets provide a means of developing speaking and listening skills. The performance may be given to oneself, or to the familiar audience of a friend or a larger group. The fun and excitement of puppetry provide an ideal play situation for participation by children who are learning English as a second language, or by children who are withdrawn or have a poor command of the language. Puppets may be used to teach children another language, such as simple conversational French. Circle time provides an excellent opportunity for encouraging participation with puppets, since each child can maintain face to face contact and relate to all the others in the group.

Children love making puppets. They provide an unrivalled visual stimulus in the classroom for motivating and stimulating language.

Lilian Coppock

(NOTE: Detailed features of hair, faces and clothes for puppets in this book have not been closely specified, so the children can devise their own characters.)

GETTING STARTED

It is important to build up a large collection of materials, including:
- junk of all types: sponges, balls, mops, scourers, tubes, boxes, cotton reels, paper plates, yoghurt pots, plastic bottles, matchboxes, corks
- braids, raffia, wool, string, feathers, fur
- buttons, beads, sequins, bottletops, pipe cleaners
- wallpapers, wrapping papers, foils, sticky labels, Cellophane, doilies, thick and thin card
- fabrics, nets, felts, lace, cotton wool, cut-off sleeves, old gloves and socks
- dowelling, garden canes, lolly sticks.

A strong initial influence gives the children plenty of ideas to work from. For example, a child may bring a puppet to school, leading to a class collection. A television programme or live puppet show may light the initial spark. Many puppeteers will come into schools and give shows and workshops, etc.

Ken Dalston's "put together, take-apart" dog is a perfect introductory stimulus to excite a child's interest, and is easy to show to the children.

You will need
a piece of white towelling
a white glove
a strip of fur for the ears
2 elastic bands and a bulldog clip
felt scraps for the eyes and tongue
       (double-sided tape on the back)
black plastic lid for the nose

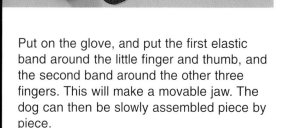

Put on the glove, and put the first elastic band around the little finger and thumb, and the second band around the other three fingers. This will make a movable jaw. The dog can then be slowly assembled piece by piece.

The children are intrigued as they gradually realise what is being made. Now the dog can bark, pant, turn his head, obey or disobey instructions, pick up a bone, do tricks, etc.

First puppets need to be quickly made so that they can be used straight away. Simple sock, stick or paper bag puppets are ideal, needing minimal help. Children will benefit from time spent in observation and discussion of features, expression and movement. They should be aware of the need for bright colours and large features. Encourage the children to explore ideas imaginatively and brainstorm ways in which a basic puppet type might be varied to create different characters, keeping ideas flexible. Choose the type of puppet that is the appropriate size, with the freedom of movement to do what is required:

      - hand or finger puppet   - marionette or string puppet
      - rod or stick puppet   - shadow puppet.

HAND AND FINGER PUPPETS

Finger Puppets

Every Early Years classroom should have an interesting box of finger puppets for the monologues that young children give when playing on their own, or in an imaginative world with others. Finger puppets are marvellous for early language and finger rhymes, and have the added advantage that several can be operated simultaneously by one person, so a whole story can be acted out. Puppets might be:-

- drawn straight on to the fingers
- drawn on card tubes
- made with Plasticine heads
- made by stitching a tube of felt **(see photograph)** and decorating to make a wide range of characters
- fingers cut off a glove and decorated
- made from a cone of felt or paper (mouse or hedgehog)
- attached to the five fingers of a glove
- drawn on to card with two holes cut out for the fingers to go through.

Hand Puppets

These are probably the most familiar type of puppet for young children, including favourites such as Sooty, and Punch and Judy. The head can be part of the fabric of the body, or can be made separately from any number of materials. The traditional felt design shown here has asymmetrical arms, to give a neat fit to the hand, and can be decorated to make a large variety of characters (as shown in photograph). Hand puppets might also be made from:

- socks or gloves
- paper bags or envelopes
- boxes, cones or plastic bottles, large enough for a hand inside
- yoghurt pots or eggboxes for talking types
- sleeves or long stitched tubes for crocodiles, birds and snakes
- tubes held vertically for a person or horizontally for an animal.

Bodies could be stretchy, bendy, flexible cloth or decorated card with the hand behind.

Sock puppets have a wide range of movement, and traditional glove puppets are the only type with the flexibility to pick up items, throw things at the audience and engage in slapstick. They have very good freedom of movement, and can bow, turn and nod their head, wave, clap, cry and rub their eyes, tip forward to look at the audience, go to sleep, dance, throw up their hands in surprise, and do useful activities such as sweeping the floor, writing a letter, or answering the phone.

STICK PUPPETS

A simple head on a stick is one of the easiest stick puppets for young children to operate. The head could be a rubber ball, a potato, a sponge, a piece of polystyrene, a box, plastic bottle or a stuffed sock end.
The lion (above) has a cheesebox head and a gathered crêpe paper body; the teddy has a cereal box head and a card body covered with fur; and the elephant has a ball of paper for the head covered with a circle of fabric secured at the neck with a rubber band.

The stick may be attached as a central rod under the head, and a shoulder piece may be added, on which to attach the arms and costume. The stick may be attached at the side for slide-on puppets, or at the back for dancing or bouncing puppets. Two sticks may be needed to operate a creeping snake or caterpillar, or a prancing horse or wolf, or a man and his boat. Several items can be operated together on one stick: for example, the 'Three Blind Mice,' or a row of brooms in 'The Sorcerer's Apprentice'.

Rods are good for pop-ups, Jack-in-the-boxes, and puppets requiring neck movements. They make excellent flying puppets such as fairies or butterflies, and if a glove is incorporated (see page 19), they can point, grasp and be very flexible. They may be used in conjunction with glove puppets in a performance. Rod puppets can be very large and dramatic, and can twirl, move at speed and be tossed into the air. Alternatively, they may be very small lolly-stick puppets. They could be reversible, with a face at the front and back, as two characters in a story, or reversible upside-down (see page 64).

Rod puppets can be very sophisticated, and may require more than one operator: one controls the central rod which turns the head and moves the puppet on and off the stage; the second operator controls sticks attached to the hands, so the puppet can salute, wave, fold his arms, etc. Javanese dancing puppets have hands that can be controlled by sticks to make beautiful and intricate dance patterns. Bunraku puppets from Japan are half life-size, with legs, and are operated by rods held in front of the puppeteers, who are shrouded in black.

STRING PUPPETS

String puppets vary enormously in size and complexity, from the simple one-stringed puppets of India to the more complex five to nine-stringed puppets in the West; to the traditional Chinese puppets which have between thirteen and thirty-six strings.

Colourful, extremely complicated stringed Kat Putli puppets from Rajasthan are used in performances of the Ramayana and Mahabharata.

A simple one-string puppet need be little more than a head on a string.

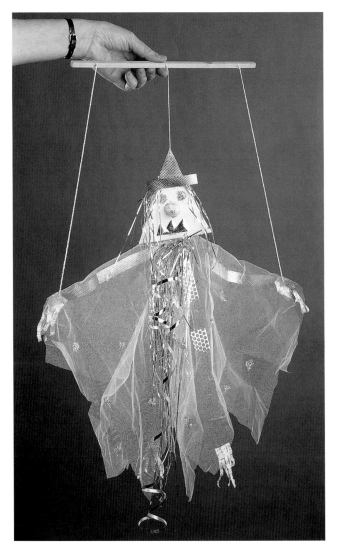

The little man in the photograph above is made from baked salt dough, with an opened paperclip (for attaching the string) pushed into the top before baking. A head could be made from any number of materials - a flowerpot, card tube, sponge, box, ball, shuttlecock, etc. Legs and arms could be anything from zigzag-folded card to felt, string, fabric or paper tubes. Heavy feet could be added if you want the puppet to clump along. Very young children find a loop of string easy to control (see page 45). Several one-string items can be attached to a single control, for example, a shoal of fish or a choir of angels.

String puppets are marvellous for flying and gliding movements (dancers, ghosts, witches, birds, fish, insects, prowling wolf, etc.), and are also very effective for bouncing and jumping movements, especially if elastic is used instead of string.

Two strings can be used to give simple articulation to a snake's body, or a duck's neck (see page 34), or a snapping mouth (see page 44).

The simple-to-control three string type shown in the photograph allows Jack Frost to move his arms and dance to spiky, frosty music. He is made from nets, tinsel and glittery oddments.

Four strings will control a dancing bird, which walks by rocking the control frame. Five strings will be needed for a figure to move all its arms and legs. Up to three strings can be attached to a simple straight control such as a piece of dowelling or a coathanger, but four or five strings will need a crossed frame control.

SHADOW PUPPETS

'The Owl who was Afraid of the Dark' - **see below**

Shadow puppets have traditionally been used for story-telling in India, China, Java and the Middle East, often accompanied by ritual song and dance. Every Indian village would have its story-teller, who told of the life of Krishna, or the deeds and legends of the great Indian hero, Prince Ram, the noblest and kindest of men. Shadow puppeteers depict stories of gods, kings and warriors, or the everyday tales of rich and poor, merchants, villains and money-lenders. The very large shadow puppets of Andhra Pradesh take three people to manipulate each one, and often show stories from Hindu mythology. Islamic shadow theatre is frequently based on the lives of holy men and saints, and is a means of moral and religious instruction. Burma, Thailand and Java have outstandingly beautiful shadow puppets, and the puppet master is regarded as a wise man. The legendary stories teach young people the religious, moral and historical traditions of the country, while images of the Gods move and answer questions.

The Greek shadow theatre uses a set of traditional characters, chief of whom is Karaghiozi, a comic hero forever trying to find food for himself and his large family.

Any dramatic stories involving night-time, monsters, wolves, dragons, knights, dinosaurs, witches, and so on, lend themselves well to a shadow performance, as in the familiar story ***The Owl who was afraid of the Dark* by J. Tomlinson (Methuen/Young Puffin), shown in the photograph above.** The outlines here are simple-to-operate cut-outs with one stick. Holes may be cut or punched out, and covered with Cellophane or coloured tissue paper. Two children can play out the action behind the screen, as it is narrated. (For details of the screen shown above, see page 70.)

The shadow may be articulated by using split pins, with one stick attached to the main body, and a second stick attached to the part you wish to move: people can talk or dance, jaws can snap, tails can lash, wings can flap.

Shadow puppets can be excitingly mixed with a hand puppet story production, with a dream sequence shown on a background shadow screen. Shadow puppets are the only ones that can leap into the air, and magically disappear.

DEVELOPING EARLY LANGUAGE

COUNTING RHYMES

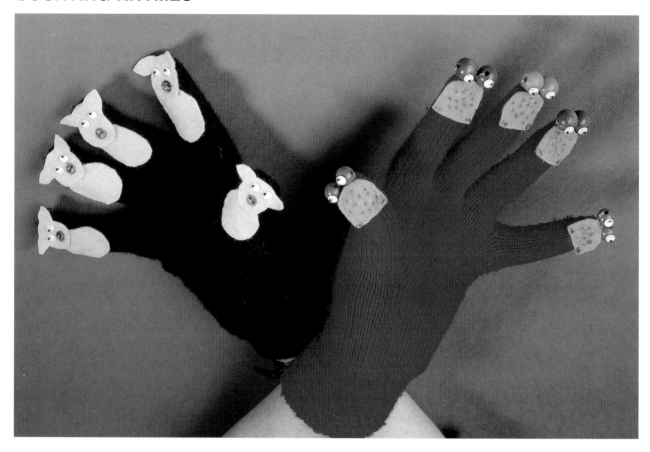

Counting is one of the earliest skills learned by second language children, and there is a variety of finger rhymes and songs that lead naturally to making puppets. One easy technique is to attach a puppet to each finger of a glove, so fingers can be added or taken away as the rhyme progresses. A puppet may be stitched or glued to the ends of the fingers, and a bank of rhymes can then be built up. Alternatively, felt puppets may be attached to the finger ends with Velcro, and moved as the rhyme dictates. Little animals or people can be simply made, using one glove for rhymes to five, and two gloves for rhymes to ten, and are excellent for use at circle time.

This little pig went to market,
This little pig stayed at home,
This little pig had roast beef,
This little pig had none.
This little pig cried "wee wee wee,
I can't find my way home."

Five little speckled frogs
Sat on a speckled log
Eating some most delicious bugs, yum-yum.
One fell into the pool
Where it was nice and cool
Then there were four green speckled frogs,
glub-glub.   etc.

Here is the beehive,
Where are the bees?
Living inside where nobody sees.
Soon they come creeping
Out of the hive
One and two and three, four, five.

Five little ducks went swimming one day
Over the pond and far away,
Mother duck said "Quack quack quack quack"
But only four little ducks came back.
                                    etc.

MORE COUNTING RHYMES

One elephant went out to play
Upon a spider's web one day.
He found it such enormous fun,
That he called for another elephant to come.

Two elephants went out to play...
        etc.

(Okki-Tokki-Unga)

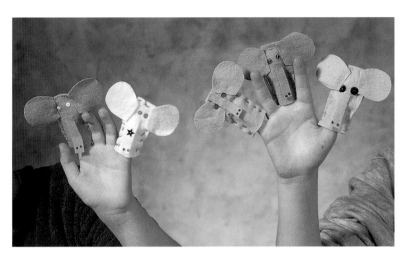

Finger puppets can be made individually and operated by one person, or by a group working together.

Co-operative tasks, where language is used in a social context, is especially valuable for children learning a second language, and the visual input of puppets will encourage participation. Puppets may be drawn straight on to fingers with non-toxic felt-tip pens, or made with felt, cloth, paper, card or cut-off glove fingers.

Five little mice came out to play,
Gathering crumbs along the way,
Along came a pussycat, sleek and black,
Four little mice went scampering back.
        etc.

Two little dicky birds sitting on a wall
One named Peter, one named Paul.
Fly away Peter, fly away Paul,
Come back Peter, come back Paul.

Three little monkeys swinging from a tree
Teasing Mr Alligator 'Can't catch me!'
Along came Mr Alligator, slowly as can be
Then snap! snap! snap!
How many monkeys can you see?
        Anon

This Little Puffin has an excellent collection of counting rhymes. Some other favourites to try with puppets are: 'Five little monkeys walked along the shore'; 'Ten little squirrels sitting in a tree'; 'One man went to mow'; 'Five little sparrows sitting in a row'; 'John Brown had a little Indian'.

LOLLY-PEOPLE PLAY

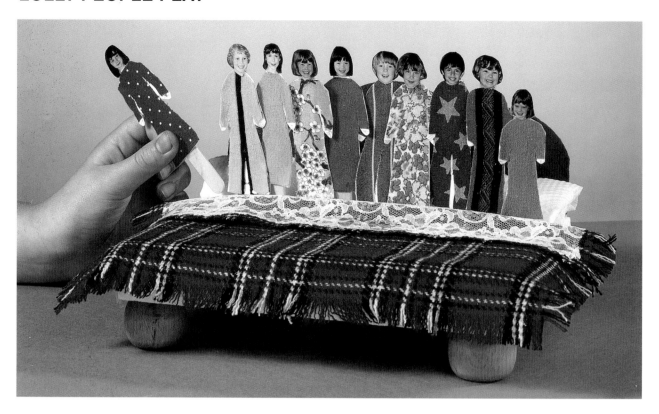

There were ten in the bed
And Sarah said 'Roll over, roll over',
So they all rolled over
and James fell out.
There were nine in the bed
And Sarah said 'Roll over, roll over',
etc.

This idea is irresistible to young children, as they love playing with puppets of themselves. From a class photograph, cut out the heads of all the children in the class, glue each one to a lolly-stick, and add pyjamas made from cloth or paper. The bed is made from a block of polystyrene, and the ten in the bed can either be laid down to sleep, or stood upright in slots made by pushing the lolly-sticks into the polystyrene. Don't forget to make a 'little one'!

Larger photographs of the children could, of course, be made into standard size puppets. These could be incorporated into stories to involve a personal element. For example, a child could become Goldilocks; or the Jolly Postman could bring letters to particular children in the class. The children will spontaneously make up conversations between two of these puppets without inhibitions.

Another use of these puppets is to choose five children to take the roles of family members - father, mother, brother, sister, baby - to act out finger rhymes such as those on page 17. An opportunity can be devised to teach the children some basic conversations between family members in another language such as French:

- *Bonjour, je m'appelle papa (or maman, le frère, la soeur, petit bébé)*
- *Bonjour, je m'apelle Sarah*
- *Bonjour, Sarah*
- *Bonjour, Papa*
- *Comment ça va, Sarah?*
- *Bien, papa*
- *Au revoir, Sarah*
- *Au revoir, Papa.*

Similar conversations can be repeated between the other family members, so the names and greetings can be learnt well.

RHYMES WITH PREPOSITIONS

Experimenting with the structure of language is a natural part of the process of learning a new language, and it is not necessary to do too much correcting in the early stages. The first essential is communication, not correctness.

Rhymes with direction words are quickly mastered, and are an enjoyable way to learn essential vocabulary.

The Jack-in-the-Box (left) is made from a ball of newspaper in the toe of a leg from a pair of tights. Push in a stick, tie at the neck, and tape the bottom edge to a box.

> Jack-in-the-box jumps up
> Jack-in-the-box jumps down
> Jack-in-the-box goes hop hop hop
> And then he turns around.

The Jack-in-the-box (right) is made by drawing a jester's head and gluing it to a strip of card. Drop this into a card tube, and stick a decorated square of card at the front. The Jack can then be popped up and down in the tube.

> Jack be nimble, Jack be quick,
> Jack jump over the candlestick.

2nd verse ends...**around** the candlestick
3rd verse ends...**behind** the candlestick
4th verse ends...**in front of** the candlestick.

> A mouse lived in a little hole
> So quietly in his little hole
> **OUT** he jumped.

2nd verse ends...**UP** he jumped
3rd verse ends...**DOWN** he jumped
4th verse ends...**AROUND** he jumped
5th verse ends...**IN** he jumped.

MORE RHYMES WITH PREPOSITIONS

A snake he likes to wiggle waggle
Wiggle waggle, wiggle waggle.
A snake he likes to wiggle waggle
Down upon the ground.

2nd verse ends...up above your head.
3rd verse ends...right in front of you.

(to the tune of 'London Bridge is Falling Down')

A hungry snake in the grass am I,
Creeping low and creeping high.
In and out the grass I go,
Up and down and to and fro.
I swallow mice and rabbits too
Look OUT, or I might swallow YOU!

Snake puppets can be made very easily by the youngest children, from socks, or by cutting off sleeves. They can also be articulated, as in the photographs above.

First snake: Made by threading balls of cotton wool together, and gluing on details and two control sticks.
Second snake: Made from lots of plastic lids punched with a central hole, and threaded with a cotton reel head, and with beads for the eyes and tail. Add a loop of thread for the control.
Third snake: Made by alternately threading mini yoghurt pots and beads. Tape on two sticks.

Other ideas for snakes with good movement include: threaded beads, cotton reels, paper cups or egg-box sections; folded paper zigzags or paper loops glued together; lots of circles joined with split pins for articulation; a piece of stocking, stuffed with paper, with elastic bands around it at intervals; a piece of skipping rope with a bead head.

Repetitive stories are an excellent way to reinforce directional language, and one of the very best is *Bears in the Night* by Stan and Jan Berenstain (Collins). Little finger puppets can be made to accompany a reading of the story, either on tape or by the teacher. The children can then move the puppet with the story line.

NURSERY RHYMES

Humpty is simply made from an oval of white card decorated with felt-tip pens and cut in half. Add paper arms and legs. He can then be whole at the beginning of the rhyme, and broken as the rhyme is read.

Humpty Dumpty sat on a wall,
Humpty Dumpty had a great fall.
All the King's horses and all the King's men,
Couldn't put Humpty together again.

Miss Muffet is made by pushing a wooden spoon into a central slit in a large circle of cloth, and then taping securely on the underside of the cloth, to make the neck.

The spider is made from a pair of black gloves. Cut the fingers off one glove (use these for other puppets), stuff the remaining piece with cotton wool and shape it into a ball. Stitch the ball securely to the back of the other glove.

Incy Wincy Spider climbed up the water spout,
Down came the rain and washed the spider out.
Out came the sun and dried up all the rain,
And Incy Wincy Spider climbed up the spout again.

Little Miss Muffet sat on a tuffet
Eating her curds and whey.
There came a big spider,
That sat down beside her,
And frightened Miss Muffet away.

RHYME SEQUENCES

Using shadow puppets is an excellent way to reinforce the correct sequence of action in a nursery rhyme.

Two children will enjoy working together behind a shadow screen to tell the story, using easy-to-operate shadow cut-outs on a stick.

> Hey diddle diddle,
> The cat and the fiddle,
> The cow jumped over the moon,
> The little dog laughed to see such fun,
> And the dish ran away with the spoon.

Some other rhymes with a clear sequence of action to try are:

- 'Sing a song of sixpence'
- 'There was an old woman who lived in a shoe'
- 'There was a crooked man'
- 'The house that Jack built'
- 'Humpty Dumpty'
- 'Little Miss Muffet'
- 'Three Blind Mice'

If several characters need to come on together (for example, the King's horses and men, or the three blind mice), they can all be operated on one stick **(see illustration).**

Sets of finger puppets are also an excellent way of encouraging children to practise and learn nursery rhyme sequences together. A set of five for each story could either be told by one child or by a group of five children working co-operatively. Some useful sets to try are:

- 'Three Blind Mice'. Make three finger mice, a farmer and his wife.
- 'Humpty Dumpty'. Make one Humpty, two horses and two King's men.
- 'Three Little Kittens'. Make three kittens, a mother cat and a father cat.
- 'Mary, Mary'. Make Mary, one set of silver bells, one set of cockle shells and two pretty maids.

ACTION RHYMES

A wide variety of amusing puppets can be made by cutting two or four holes in a card outline, for fingers.

The fingers may become legs on a snowman, clown, ballerina or animal; they could be ears for a rabbit or vampire bat, or eyes for a space alien or monster.

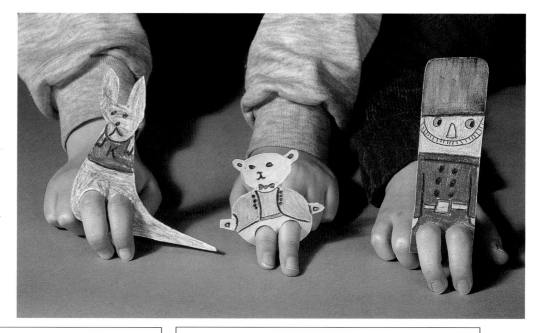

Teddy bear, teddy bear, turn around,
Teddy bear, teddy bear, touch the ground,
Teddy bear, teddy bear, show your shoe,
Teddy bear, teddy bear, that will do!

etc.

We are the soldiers, marching along,
Left right, left right, left right, left right.
Waving the flag as we march, march along,
Left right, left right, HALT!

Try also (from *This Little Puffin*) : 'Jump, Jump, Kangaroo Brown', 'Ten galloping horses' and 'Ladybird, ladybird, fly away home'.

Finger puppets of people (drawn on simple card tubes - **see photograph**) form the basis of play in a large number of different action rhymes.

Tommy Thumb, Tommy Thumb,
Where are you?
Here I am, here I am, how do you do.

Repeat with other fingers: Peter Pointer, Toby Tall, Ruby Ring, Baby Small, Fingers all.

Here is the father short and stout,
Here is the mother with children all about,
Here is the brother tall you see,
Here is the sister with dolly on her knee,
Here is the baby sure to grow,
And here is the family, all in a row.

HANDS AND FEET ACTION

A simple face on a hand cut-out makes an excellent puppet. It may be drawn straight on to the hand shape, front facing or side facing; it may be a card cut-out; it may be stuck on to a glove, or a little face attached with tape.

The hand can move to the song 'One day a hand went walking'; it can walk, hop and turn, quickly or slowly.

'One day a hand went walking......' (from _BBC Playschool Publications_)

Roly poly, ever so slowly,
Ever.....so.....slowly.....
Ever.....so.....slowly
Roly poly, ever, so quickly, etc.

(using two hands)

Turn around and touch the ground (three times)
And fall right down.

Make up your own verses:
- _Turn around and nod your head_
- _Turn around and hop along, etc._

(Photograph left)
This is great fun! Draw around your shoes, cut out and decorate with faces, and attach to the shoe with tape. The children can lie on the floor with their feet on a low bench and enjoy all kinds of stomping, marching, rhythmic rhymes and songs. Try:
- 'Grand Old Duke of York'
- 'Here we go Looby Loo'
- 'Cobbler, cobbler, mend my shoe'
- 'We are the soldiers' (or 'children') - see previous page.

I can run in trainers,
In trainers, in trainers,
I can run in trainers,
All around the room.

(to the tune of 'Aiken Drum')
Try other verses -
creep in slippers,
stamp in wellies,
etc.

I went to school one morning and I walked like this,
Walked like this, walked like this,
I went to school one morning and I walked like this,
On my way to school.

Continue with other verses: _hopped, stamped, ran,_ etc.

POINTING PUPPETS - FOR LEARNING A SECOND LANGUAGE

Many children learning another language will need a long period of listening and understanding before they attempt to speak. Simple puppet play between the child and teacher, or within a small group of children, can be directed to reinforce newly learned vocabulary and encourage a verbal response.

The pointing puppet, shown here, is a stimulating encouragement for children whose understanding of a new language is developing well, but whose confidence at speaking needs some support.

Withdrawn or language-reluctant children will also benefit from participating in puppet games.

To make the clown: tape a stick to a paper plate, push the stick through a central slit in a large circle of cloth, and tape securely underneath. Make another slit at the side of the cloth, wider than a glove, and sew the glove inside the slit.

These puppets can wave, shake hands or look thoughtful, and they are excellent for games involving pointing, throwing and picking up.

Pointing ideas
The teacher may direct the conversation if the child is learning numbers, shapes, colours, classroom objects, etc. The child/puppet points and repeats the word.
- Point to something red (blue, green)
- Point to something square (round, triangular)
- Point to something big (little, long, thin)
- Point to the table (pencil, scissors, chair)
- Point to my nose (hair, leg, eyes).

Throwing ideas
The child/puppet may have a selection of soft toys, beanbags or dolls' clothes in front of him, to be thrown to children in a group. This is also good for learning children's names - and catching practice!
- Throw the square beanbag to James
- Thrown the little teddy to Joanna
- Throw the blue dress to Jack.

Picking-up ideas
- How many pencils can you pick up?
- Can your puppet make a tower of five bricks? Can he put ten blue beads in a box?
- 'Where is the red one?' game: The puppet has three bricks (red, yellow, blue), and three boxes to hide them under. Puppeteer puts a brick under each box, slides the boxes around quickly, and asks the audience 'Where is the red brick?

SPEAKING AND LISTENING GAMES

These hilarious puppets are fun to make and operate, and will generate enthusiasm in the shyest children.

Children thoroughly enjoy hammering details of a face (beads, buttons, sprouts, split pins, felt scraps, etc., held on with nails) into a turnip, bumpy potato or wrinkled apple. (These make excellent witches, owls or hedgehogs, too.)

'I'm a dingle dangle scarecrow with a flippy floppy hat
I can shake my hands like this, and shake my feet like that.'

For younger children, a simple body can be made by gluing a strip of card to a control stick, to make a crossbar over which an oddment of sacking may be draped. Push the top into the potato.

Older children may want the head to move independently of the body, so it can swivel and go up and down. For this, push a piece of stick through the top of a kitchen roll tube to make the crossbar. The control stick can then be dropped through, with the head attached.

Yes or No Games

The teacher chooses a category of questions, and gives the children some examples to get them started. The puppet has to answer Yes or No to questions from the children, the sillier the better. (The swivel version can also move its head.) For example:

Body	**Food**	**Silly**
- Do you have two noses?	- Do you like to eat soap?	- Can a fish fly?
- Do you have three legs?	- Do you like cake?	- Can a bus swim?
- Do you have one hand?	- Do you like to eat trees?	- Can a cat drive a car?

'Make that Noise' Game

The teacher tells the children that the puppet is going to make noises, and they have to guess what they are. If the puppeteer needs help, the teacher may whisper instructions or give him a set of picture cards to choose from. For example: **animal noises** (frog, cat, dog, farm animal); **indoor noises** (sausages cooking, clock, fridge, phone, doorbell, hinges creaking); **outdoor noises** (bees, birds, wind, rain, aeroplane, fire engine, feet clumping).

LISTENING TO INSTRUCTIONS

Using a robot and controller is an excellent way to encourage children to listen carefully to instructions, to carry them out, and to give clear spoken instructions. The controller tells the robot what to do, and this can be simple tasks such as:

- Go quickly or slowly forwards, backwards; three steps to the left.

- Go upstairs, downstairs; hop, dance, walk.

- Sing 'Humpty Dumpty'.

The controller could give precise instructions on how to perform a task, such as how to thread a needle, or tie shoelaces, or do a jigsaw, or make a sandwich.

The controller could tell the audience that the robot is very good and clever, and does just what he is told. This opens the opportunity for slapstick when the robot makes mistakes, counts wrongly, goes the wrong way, sings the wrong song, and so on.

The controller could instruct the robot to 'go and get a ....', giving the robot the opportunity to go off-stage to collect a prop. This might be a basket hung over its arm, or a card cut-out moved on a stick, or a card outline with Velcro on the back attached to Velcro on the robot's 'hand'.

For example:
- Give the robot a broom and tell it to sweep the floor. (It might then sweep the ceiling or the controller.)
- Give the robot a paintbrush and tell it to paint the wall. (It might paint the controller instead.)
- Tell the robot to bring a basket of apples. It might bring back a basket with a snake in it (on a stick) which chases the controller.

Some other games to play might be 'Controller Says' (i.e. Simon Says), or the 'Changing Voices' game, where the robot has to say a phrase such as 'I am a robot' in the voice indicated by the controller. This could be *quietly, loudly, in a whisper, quickly, very slowly*; it could be in an *angry, happy, sad, sleepy, scared* or *excited* voice; or in the voice of a witch, giant, snake, very old man, or ROBOT!

EXTENDING VOCABULARY AND ORAL CONFIDENCE

CHARACTER PUPPETS

Character puppets are always popular with young children, and can appear on stage by themselves or with another character, so that they can have a conversation.

The princess (above) is simply made by gluing a stick into a sponge head and adding a dress of crêpe paper and lace. **The space monster's head** is a kitchen scourer, and the body is a plastic bag. These two characters might have a conversation about where they come from, what their home is like, what they like to eat, or wear, or do. The teacher, or a confident child, may 'interview' them using a microphone, and prompting with specific questions. Audience participation can also be encouraged by getting the children to ask them questions.

Characters from real life might talk about their role:
- a lollipop lady telling how to cross the road safely
- a policeman telling you how to catch a robber
- a clown telling jokes or tongue-twisters
- a fireman telling you how to put out a fire
- a deep sea diver telling you about life at the bottom of the sea
- a spaceman talking about how to fly a rocket to the moon.

Characters from familiar stories can also be encouraged to speak:
- Red Riding Hood tells you what is in her basket, and why.
- Brer Fox tells you what he will do to Brer Rabbit when he catches him (*Brer Rabbit* by Joel Chandler Harris, Pelham Books).
- The Jolly Postman tells you who he will deliver letters to (*The Jolly Postman* by J & A Ahlberg, Heinemann).
- Rosie tells about her walk round the farmyard (*Rosie's Walk* by Pat Hutchins, Picture Puffin).
- Mrs Lather tells you how to wash clothes (*Mrs Lather's Laundry* by A. Ahlberg, Puffin).

USING A TELEVISION SCREEN

A television screen gives the puppet an opportunity to be a presenter, a news reporter, a dancer or an entertainer. The screen above is made from three pieces of stiff card, taped to make hinged sides, with a hole cut for the screen. The screen area can be reinforced by gluing four strips of dowelling at the back (it will have lots of wear!). The whole thing stands on a table-top. Make sure the screen is large enough for two puppets to perform together, or for the puppet to appear with the operator, so they can have a conversation.

The chef in the photograph above, has gloves inserted into the fabric body (as on page 19), so he can pick up a spoon or ingredients, scratch, throw pepper about, explain how to make a cake, gesticulate wildly, and so on. The head is made from a one-litre plastic drinks bottle: cut off the top one-third (for the neck) and the bottom one-third (for the head) and discard the middle. Make a few snips on the neck part so the two sections of bottle slide into each other, and secure with clear adhesive tape. The bottle may be left clear, brown or green, or it may be made flesh-coloured by covering with the end of a stocking. Tape a circle of white cloth to the neck, put a finger in the neck to control the puppet, and one hand in one of the gloves.

Other ideas for a television programme might be:

- a footballer talking about the match
- a pop star talking about his latest song
- the weatherman giving tomorrow's weather
- a guitarist 'playing' to taped music
- a class reporter visiting another class for ten minutes, and reporting on everything he saw
- ideas on how to amuse yourself in bed when you are ill.

TALKING PUPPETS

These are two ideas for puppets where the mouth actually moves - the child simply *has* to talk when operating them. (For other ideas, see pages 41 and 62.)

For the talking heads (above), first practise drawing profiles with big noses, mouths and chins. Then draw and cut out a head on black card, with a nice big jaw section. Cut off the jaw, and attach the two pieces with a split pin, so that the jaw will pivot. Tape a stick to the back of each piece of card.

For the giant (right), cut two fingerholes above the hinged side of an egg box, so the mouth will move when you move your hand. Cut out and paint a large head from card, cut it in half and glue the halves to the front parts of the egg box. Glue a piece of stiff card under the egg box for the shoulders, and hang wallpaper clothes on this.

SOMETHING TO TALK ABOUT

Using a telephone as a prop encourages children to articulate clearly in a familiar context. Role play builds confidence, and children are less inhibited about expressing their ideas and feelings when talking through a puppet. The phone can be a cardboard cut-out held for the puppet by the puppeteer, or it can be taped to the puppet's hand; but if you want the puppet to pick up the phone and dial numbers, you will need a glove puppet.

A leather or woollen glove can be made into a versatile range of picking-up puppets, using the index finger as the neck, and the thumb and middle fingers for arms. The head could be a matchbox **(as above)**; a rubber ball with a hole in it; a small plastic bottle; a card tube; or a stuffed toe piece of a sock gathered at the neck. The head can be painted, or covered with a small piece of sock or tights. You might add a tie, a necklace or a skirt. If desired, the two unused fingers of the glove can be cut off and stitched up.

If you provide two telephones, children will spontaneously make up their own conversations, between two puppets, or a puppeteer and another child. The teacher may give the puppet a message to deliver:
- Phone the fire brigade because the house next door is on fire.
- Phone Grandma and tell her what you've been doing at school.
- Phone your friend to invite him to tea, and tell him what there is to eat.
- Phone the doctor to come and visit because Teddy is sick.

Some other things to talk about:
- three wishes you would like to make
- something you are afraid of
- food you don't like
- your best friend, brother or sister
- what makes you really sad or happy or angry.

Opposites puppets can be made, such as Mr Happy and Mr Sad, Mr Silly and Mr Sensible, or Mr Kind and Mr Mean. Interesting telephone conversations can develop as the puppeteers try to empathise with their character and speak appropriately. (NOTE: This idea also works well with reversible stick puppets, with a happy face on one side and a sad face on the other.)

CONVERSATIONS

Puppets with waving arms or wings are fun to make, and reinforce the essential rule that the puppet needs to move when it is talking, so the audience knows which character is speaking.

To make the cone body, cut out a one-third segment from a 25cm diameter circle, and staple. You will need three strips of stiff card for the moving mechanism, held together with a split pin (see drawing). Make slots in opposite sides of the cone and push the arms through the slots from inside the cone. Moving the central strip of card up and down will lower and raise the arms.

Now decorate as you wish - you may like to try a policeman, robber, pirate or scarecrow.

The characters shown in the photograph may wish to talk about:

- how to make magic potions and spells
- the best spell I ever made
- how my spell went wrong
- what I would do if I lost my magic wand
- what I would do if I got lost while flying at night.

The teacher might pose 'helping' problems for the puppets. For example, how would they help if:

- a cat is stuck in a tree
- a crocodile has toothache
- a man is out fishing and a shark appears
- a mouse is in a hole and a cat wants it
- a family has lost its door key
- one child has two sweets and his friend has none.

POP-UPS AND DESCRIBING GAMES

FROSTIE THE SNOWMAN
The head is a painted ball on a stick. The body is made from a folded square of felt stitched at the sides.

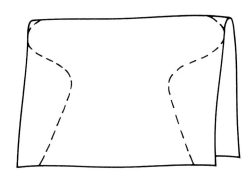

Make the cone from a quarter segment of a circle of card. Glue the felt body to the top of the cone and to the base of the head. The stick, pushed up through the cone and into the head, controls the puppet.

SANTA IN THE CHIMNEY
Make the head from two circles of felt, lightly stuffed. The chimney is a sponge-printed length of card, folded into a box shape.

Other heads to try:-
- a coffee jar lid
- a ball of Plasticine
- a wooden spoon.

'Who am I?' describing game
- 'This person has short, curly black hair and his name begins with *T*.'
- Father Christmas describes a child who has been very good.
- The Snowman describes the child he would like to fly with to Snowman land.
- A pop-up pirate might describe the child he would make walk the plank.
- A pop-up crocodile might describe the child he would like to eat.

'Stop and Start' singing
The children all sing a Christmas carol or song when the pop-up puppet is out, and stop every time he goes back in.

CIRCLE TIME

ALPHABET PUPPETS

Various types of paper bag puppets can be made with a letter of the alphabet on them such as (shown in the photographs) **f, b, m and c** - frog, bird, monkey and cat. Some bags have a fold, so the puppet can 'talk'; or they can be stuffed with newspaper to make them three-dimensional.

Phonic games for circle time

- Make the appropriate animal noise when the teacher holds up your letter.
- All puppets beginning with 'C' take turns to name something they like to eat (*crisps, cookies, cauliflower, cucumber,*) or do (*crawl, climb, cook*).
- The teacher calls out descriptive words such as *mischievous, magical*, and (in this case) all the *monkeys* have to make a noise and jump about.
- Sing the alphabet together, and hold up your puppet when you get to your letter.

Other circle games to try

- Pass around a giant or spider puppet: each child says what the puppet would like for dinner. Responses could be taped or made into a class poem.
- 'Getting to know you' games, where puppets take turns to speak about their owners. Positive self-awareness can be boosted by the puppets saying something they can do well.
- Silly or sensible sentences written by the children encourage careful listening. The teacher can give some examples to get them thinking, for example: *The bus hopped along the road; The goldfish read the paper.*
  The teacher reads out a sentence and, if it is sensible, the puppets applaud or bounce up and down. If it is silly they boo or fall over and laugh.

28

THE PUPPET AS THE TEACHER

This is a really quick and easy puppet, made from an old stuffed toy such as a dog or a teddy. Unpick the back seam and remove the stuffing so your hand will fit inside. The arms can be manipulated, and the puppet can pick up 3D items, nod its head, sniff, walk, sleep, etc. It is a flexible and appealing puppet and the children will enjoy miming different moods with it - being happy, sad, frightened, cold, angry, sleepy, and so on.

Sets of cards could be made, perhaps mounted on sticks, so the puppet can pick them up and choose the next one.

Games to play include:

- 'I spy', where the puppet chooses a letter of the alphabet, and the children have to guess the word. He can nod or shake his head.
- 'I spy colours', where the children have to guess the chosen classroom object.
- Puppet holds up a child's name card. It is that person's turn to sing a rhyme, tell his news, or change the weather chart.
- Number bonds give excellent quick recall practice.
- The puppet holds up the words for the next verse in a song such as 'If you're happy and you know it.'
- The puppet has a set of items on a tray beginning with *b* or *d*, and the children help it to sort the items into two sets, by initial sound.
- The puppet sorts out pairs of rhyming words helped by the children. The 'Pat the Cat' series of books by C & J Hawkins (Picture Puffins) are an excellent source of rhyming words in a story context.
- The puppet can turn the pages of a reading flip chart or move magnet-board letters to help with spelling.

SHORT RHYMES

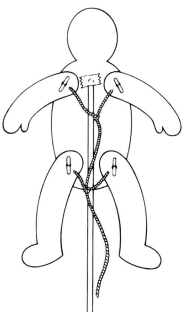

> I went for a walk in the woods today
> And what do you think I met on the way?
> I met a lion and what did he say?
> - 'Roar, roar, roar.'

Repeat with *bear, crocodile, snake,* etc.

> Bounce the ball, bounce the ball,
> Bounce the ball high.
> Now bounce gently and let the bounce die.
> Bounce the ball, bounce the ball,
> Bounce the ball low.
> Now bounce harder, and let the bounce grow.

The simple puppets (above) have Plasticine heads with a hole underneath, large enough for a finger. The bodies are stiff cones with the tops cut off.

Short rhymes are quickly learnt by young children, and can be recited individually with puppet action, or by a small group.

(Try this with a ball on a piece of elastic. You could add a funny face to make a little character.)

This Little Puffin contains many short rhymes. See 'Slowly creeps the garden snail' and 'Mr Jumping Jack Man'.

> Jumping Jack can jump like this,
> Jump like this, jump like this.
> Jumping Jack can jump like this,
> Jump, jump, jump.

(repeat with *hop, run, slide, fly, sleep,* etc.)

This short rhyme can be sung to the tune of 'London Bridge is falling down', and can be adapted for all types of puppets. For example, 'An elephant (*skeleton, wiggly worm*) can jump like this.'

Jumping Jack (left) has been made as a simple stick puppet with movable limbs.

Attach the limbs with split pins and the string as shown. Attach a stick.

Try with a teddy, a monster, a Humpty, etc.

ACTION POEMS

Read 'I am a tiger' by Mary Ann Hoberman (*A Very First Poetry Book*).

Children love puppets which allow them to growl, bite, snap and thump, and a carefully chosen poem can add to the fun.

The tiger marionette (above) is made by covering a one litre milk carton with yellow felt, and gluing on stripes of black fur. Add a plastic lid head, and felt legs. Wooden bricks for feet make a satisfying clumping noise. Add a loop of string to walk the tiger along. If you wish to articulate the head and tail, attach the head with a split pin. Then add three strings, for the head, body and tail.

Make the bodies of the goblin and crocodile from two long strips of card folded over and over to make a firm zigzag. Make arms and legs with pipe-cleaners threaded with beads, and make heads and feet with card. These puppets make an interesting rattly noise as they clump around.

If you should meet a crocodile,
Don't take a stick and poke him.
Ignore the welcome in his smile,
Be careful not to stroke him.

For as he sleeps upon the Nile,
He thinner gets, and thinner,
And whene'er you meet a crocodile
He's ready for his dinner!

Anon

Try also 'The Goblin' by Rose Fyleman, in *The Book of a Thousand Poems*.

QUESTION AND ANSWER RHYMES

Two puppets may talk together, one asking questions and one giving answers; or the audience may ask the questions and the puppet give the answers.

The flowerpot man is made from four flowerpots, with card arms, tiny fibre flowerpots for hands, and straw hair.

The doll has a floppy fabric body with thick string for arms, legs and hair, and a cotton reel head.

What's your name?	- Sarah Jane
Where do you live?	- in a sieve
What town?	- upside-down
What street?	- cat's meat
What house?	- brown mouse
What number?	- cucumber.
	Anon

Where are you going, my little pig?
I'm going to town to get me a wig.
A pig in a wig! A wig for a pig!
Whoever heard of a pig in a wig?

Where are you going, my little cat?
I'm going to town to get me a hat.
A cat in a hat! A hat for a cat!
Whoever heard of a cat in a hat?
Anon.

Other balloon characters could be:
- a fox in a box
- a hen with a pen
- a frog on a log
- kittens with mittens.

Other good rhymes to try are: 'What's the time, Mr Wolf?' and 'Rat-a-tat-tat, who is that?'

POEMS WITH DIALOGUE

To make the hen: Stitch together two pieces of yellow fabric, or use a yellow sock. Add felt details.
To make the chicks: Cut the fingertips off a yellow glove, stuff them lightly and stitch each one to the fingertips of a glove. Glue on felt details.

Read *The Chicken Book* by Garth Williams (Picture Lions).

Some suggestions for short poems containing dialogue, suitable for puppet action:

- 'Six little mice sat down to spin', in *The Book of a Thousand Poems*
- 'Witch, witch' by Rose Fyleman, *A Very First Poetry Book*
- 'Who killed Cock Robin?', Anon.
- 'Old Shellover' by Walter de la Mare, *The Book of a Thousand Poems*
- 'Puppy and I', by A.A. Milne, *The Puffin Book of 20th Century Children's Verse*
- 'Pussycat, pussycat, where have you been?', Trad.

Many longer poems with dialogue are also good for dramatising. Try:

- 'Overheard on a Saltmarsh', by Harold Monro, *The Book of a Thousand Poems*
- 'The sick young dragon', by John Foster, *A Very First Poetry Book*
- 'You were the mother last time', by Mary Ann Hoberman, *A Very First Poetry Book*
- 'My dad, your dad', by Kit Wright, *Comic Verse*
- 'The Lobster Quadrille', by Lewis Carroll, *The Oxford Book of Children's Verse*
- 'Colonel Fazackerley', by Charles Causley, *Puffin Book of 20th Century Children's Verse*
- 'The blind man and the elephant', by John Godfrey Saxe, *The Book of a Thousand Poems*
- 'King John and the Abbot of Canterbury', *The Book of a Thousand Poems.*

The poems may be read by the teacher, or put on to tape if desired. Older children may want to learn or read their speaking parts, and use a narrator for the non-speaking parts.

POEMS FOR MOVEMENT

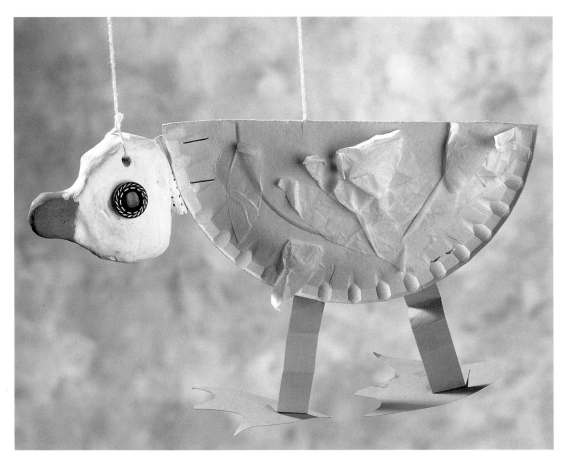

Some poetry evokes its own special atmosphere by depicting movement, maybe capering and lively, maybe peaceful and gliding. The narrator reads the poem, and the puppets can interpret the mood through their movement. The poem may be paused at any point to insert dialogue or short pieces of action from the puppets, if desired.

- 'Ducks Ditty' by Kenneth Graham (*Oxford Book of Children's Verse*) sets the scene on a still and sunny summer day, with the quiet flow of the river contrasted with the busy, purposeful dabbling of the ducks.
  The duck puppet above has a flexible neck to enable it to be 'head down, tail up'. Make the head from a flattened ball of clay with a strip of hessian pushed firmly into it for the neck. Make a hole at the top of the head to take a string. When the clay is dry, paint it and staple the neck inside a folded paper plate. Add legs, feet and feathers, and strings for the head and body.
  The background scenery could have a river at the bottom, with reeds and fish, and a blue sky above. Extra puppets could also be introduced such as roach or swifts on sticks. The children could make up some quiet, ripply music to be played before and after the poem.

- 'The Dolphin' by Alan Bold (*A Very First Poetry Book*) lends itself to a shadow puppet performance (with blue lightning) of sea creatures on the journey round the world.

- 'Hallowe'en' by Jean Kenward (*A Very First Poetry Book*) suggests you need to hurry to see all the scary, mischievous Hallowe'en characters - pixie, witch, giant, fairy, etc.

- 'Stocking and Shirt' by James Reeve (*The Wandering Moon*, Puffin) suggests a wild and windy March day, with the washing whipping about on the line, and finally blowing away.
  A shirt, petticoat, skirt, and so on, could be cut out from cloth and attached to sticks, so they can dance, 'minuet' and 'pirouette' away, waving goodbye as they go.

Short atmospheric poems can sometimes be used very effectively to set the mood before a performance (spooky, dreamy, lively, etc.).

POEMS WITH A STORY

The famous tale of 'The Owl and the Pussycat' by Edward Lear (*The Oxford Book of Children's Verse*) is a classic for dramatising. There is a simple storyline, just four basic characters, and a party at the end. Props on sticks can be inserted into the action - a guitar, fishes during the voyage, and bong trees. It could begin with a sea shanty before the poem, a little guitar music after the first verse, and a minuet or barn dance music at the end. Make the puppets from two pieces of card laced together through holes punched around the edge, and painted with inks and glitter paints. The beautiful pea-green boat is a stand-up model that can be removed after verse one.

Some other suggestions for poems with a good storyline, suitable for dramatising with puppets:

- 'The house that Jack built' (*Book of a Thousand Poems*)
- 'The boy and the snake' by Charles and Mary Lamb (*Oxford Book of Children's Verse*)
- 'The King's Breakfast' by A.A.Milne (*Oxford Book of Children's Verse*)
- 'Adventures of Isabel' by Ogden Nash (*Puffin Book of 20th Century Children's Verse*)
- *Revolting Rhymes* by Roald Dahl (Picture Puffins) - especially 'Snow White'
- 'The old wife and the ghost' by James Reeve (*The Wandering Moon*)
- 'The story of Jackie Thimble' by James Reeve (*The Wandering Moon*).

Many poems with a story have a strong moral element, and you may wish to dramatise one of these to reinforce a particular message, or to use in a school assembly. Try:

- 'The Pied Piper of Hamelin' by Robert Browning (*Oxford Book of Children's Verse*)
- 'The Story of Johnny Head in air' by Heinrich Hoffmann (*Oxford Book of Children's Verse*)
- 'Two little kittens', Anon. (*Oxford Book of Children's Verse*)
- 'The Country Mouse and the City Mouse' by Richard Sharpe (*Oxford Book of Children's Verse*)
- 'The Mouse, the Frog, and the Little Red Hen', Anon. (*Early Years Rhymes and Poems*).

SONGS AND MUSIC

SONGS THAT TELL A STORY

Songs that tell a story may be sung by the class or acted out to a tape as the story unfolds. Children quickly learn to operate a tape recorder by themselves, and will enjoy playing out the action over and over to a taped story.

The three little pigs, above, are standard felt finger puppets. The wolf's head is cut out from black plastic foam or card, cut in half along the jaw-line. To make the wolf's jaw move, so he can snap up the pigs, you will need eight lolly-sticks, each punched with three holes by a heavy-duty hole punch. Fix the sticks together with split pins, and glue the end two sticks to the halves of the head.
The houses are card cut-outs on sticks, so the pigs can look out of the door and windows at the wolf.

(NOTE: This opening and closing jaw mechanism is also excellent for snapping dinosaurs and crocodiles. Traditional Indian puppets have cobra heads, and can be used for striking out very quickly.)

Songs with a good story-line, suitable for puppetry, include:

- 'There was a princess long ago' (*This Little Puffin*)
- 'When Goldilocks went to the house of the bears' (*Okki-Tokki-Unga*)
- 'Froggie went a courting and he did ride' (*Apusskidu*)
- 'There's a little white duck, swimming in the water' (*Sing a Song One*)
- 'A mouse lived in a windmill in old Amsterdam' (*Apusskidu*)
- 'Daddy's taking us to the zoo tomorrow' (*Apusskidu*)
- 'Puff the Magic Dragon' (*Sing a Song One*).

Cumulative songs: These could be acted out with each puppet in turn stepping forward as it is mentioned in the song, as in 'Old McDonald' (see facing page).

OLD McDONALD'S FARM

Old McDonald had a farm
E I E I O
And on that farm he had a sheep
E I E I O.

To make the sheep: stitch or glue an oblong of white woolly material over a dark sock, and glue on felt details.

And on that farm he had a horse
E I E I O.

To make the horse: push a paper cup into a white sock. Stitch or glue an oblong of white cloth over the sock for the body. Add felt details and a woolly mane.

And on that farm he had a pig
E I E I O.

To make the pig: glue a 5cm circle of stiff card inside the toe of a pink sock, and stitch or glue an oblong of pink cloth over the sock. The pig's nose is very animated and flexible -very good for gobbling food actions.

Other cumulative songs to try:

- 'Widdecombe Fair' (*The Music Box Songbook*)
- 'I bought me a cat' (*Silver Burdett Music,* Ginn).
- 'I know an old lady who swallowed a fly' (*Children's Funnyday Songbook*)

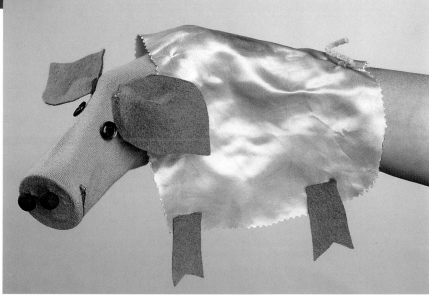

SONGS WITH ACTION

Songs to use for dinosaur shadow puppets could be:

- 'The Prehistoric Animal Brigade' (*Okki-Tokki-Unga*)
- 'When a dinosaur's feeling hungry' (*Game Songs*)

Carefully draw and cut out dinosaur outlines on black card, ensuring that the part you wish to move (head, jaw, tail, arm or wing) is not too small. Cut off the section that will move and re-attach it with a split pin so it will pivot. If desired, cut out holes or body detail and add coloured Cellophane. Tape a stick to the back of each section.

Children are very enthusiastic about acting out battles between meat-eaters and plant-eaters, and appropriate sound effects (feet stamping, scales rattling, jaws and teeth snapping, beaks clacking) can be added using percussion instruments. Get the children to choose an instrument for each dinosaur, and play it to the action, matching the sounds they make to the movements of the puppet.

Songs with simple words and a catchy tune will motivate children to join in. Children with speech hesitancy can often sing things they cannot say.

Some action songs to try with puppets might be:

- 'Walking through the jungle' (*Game Songs*)
- 'In a cottage in a wood' (*Okki-Tokki-Unga*)
- 'Six little ducks that I once knew' (*Okki-Tokki-Unga*)
- 'The birdie song' (*Children's Funnyday Songbook*)
- 'The day I went to sea' (*The Funny Family*)
- 'Put your finger on your head' (*Okki-Tokki-Unga*) - for pointing puppets
- 'Look at the terrible crocodile' (*This Little Puffin*)
- 'Witch Song' (*Sing a Song One*).

Assemblies
Some songs popular in school assemblies are excellent for dramatising with puppets. Try particularly those with a succession of animals or people, such as 'The Animals went in two by two' (*Apusskidu*) and 'How many people live in your house?' (*Tinderbox*).

STRETCH AND BEND

'Bendy Toy' (*Game Songs*) is a perfect song for these bendy, stretchy puppets to move to, and the children will enjoy copying the shapes they make.

(see photograph left)
Bendy Man can be made from any flexible materials such as plastic pipe lagging, bits of hosepipe or, as here, foam carpet underlay cut into head, body, arms and legs shapes. Staple the pieces together, and add strings to the head and arms. He is very flexible and bendy. Add a further two strings to the knees to give an extra range of movement.

'He bends over here, he bends over there'

(see photograph right)
Stretchy Man is made by folding a piece of wallpaper in half, and drawing and cutting lines on it, as shown below.

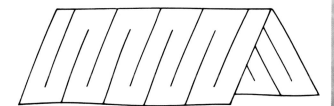

Open the paper, gently stretch it, and add a card head, hands and feet. A wooden brick glued to each foot will anchor him and make him easier to stretch. Glue a loop for holding on the back of the head.

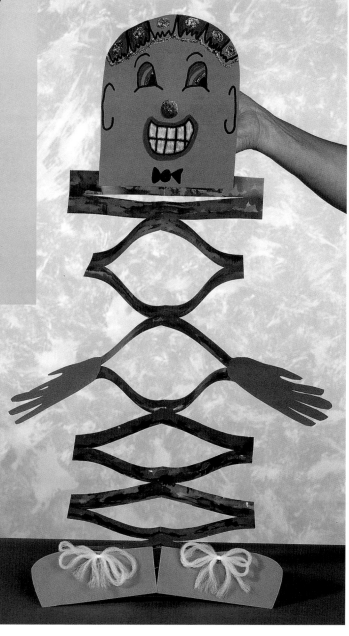

'He's a piece of elastic'

39

FLY, CREEP, JUMP AND HOP

Try these simple puppets:

Ghost: Wrap a handkerchief over a ball of cotton wool, secured at the neck with a pipe cleaner.
Jumping spider: Glue a length of elastic to a green-painted tennis ball, and attach zigzag card legs.
(This also works well with a woollen bobble.)
Butterfly (or frog): Draw the outline on marbled paper, cut out, and glue on a stick.

These and similar puppets can be used in familiar songs with actions. The words of many songs can be played around with and adapted to suit the purpose in hand. For example:

- Adapt 'The Bear went over the mountain' and sing 'The ghost flew over the castle, to see what he could see'. Other verses could be added:
    The ghost jumped over the tower; the ghost hopped over the drawbridge; the ghost howled down in the dungeons...and so on.

- Adapt 'Wiggley Woo' (*Sing a Song One*). Instead of 'There's a worm at the bottom of my garden', you could try 'a snake (slug, snail, etc) at the bottom of my garden'.

- Make up new action words to a familiar tune such as 'Twinkle Twinkle Little Star':
    'Hop spider, hop spider, hop a little then,
    Creep spider, creep spider, stop and start again.'
Other verses could be added:
    'Jump spider....then dance spider'; 'Walk spider...then sleep spider'...and so on.

Some other popular movement songs to try:-
    'Inchworm' (*Birds and Beasts*)
    'Caterpillars only crawl' (*Harlequin*)
    'The Kangaroo Song' (*Apusskidu*)
    'Fancy Anansi, clever little spider', by David Moses, African and Caribbean pack, (*Tinderbox Music*).

QUESTION AND RESPONSE SONGS

Question and answer songs enable two puppets to sing their words to each other.

Alternatively, the songs may be taped, or sung live by the class, with half the class asking the question, and the other half giving the answer, while the puppets move.

The song represented by these puppets is 'Old woman, old woman' from *Apusskidu:*

Q. 'Old woman, old woman, will you come a-shearing?'
A. 'Speak a little louder, sir, I'm rather hard of hearing.'

These very amusing 'talking and singing' puppets have heads made from yoghurt pots which have two sections. Glue or staple a large piece of cloth (about 50cmx50cm) right around the pot, starting at the side of the face. Glue on any details you wish. Make the puppet sing by putting your hand in the yoghurt pot, and opening and closing the two sections. Some other question and response songs to try:-

- 'There's a hole in my bucket, dear Liza, dear Liza' (*Apusskidu*)
- 'Do you know the Muffin Man' (*This Little Puffin*)
- 'How many people live in your house?' (*Tinderbox*)
- 'You're a pink toothbrush, I'm a blue toothbrush' (*Children's Sunnyday Songbook*)

41

DANCING TO A RHYTHMIC BEAT

Appalachian puppet (left)
These puppets are normally made of wood, but this easy version uses a stiff card body, with floppy arms and beaded legs. Glue a stick to the back of the doll.

The puppeteer sits on a flexible strip of wood extending out from the chair, with the puppet's feet just resting on the wood. The board is then banged with a fist, causing it to vibrate, and making the doll dance.

> Dance little dolly
>   with a hole in her stocking,
> Her toes keep a-tapping,
>   Her knees keep a-knocking,
> Dance little dolly
>   with a hole in her stocking,
> Dance by the light of the moon.

Dance the puppet to the song:
(to the tune of 'Buffalo girls, won't you come out tonight')

Tulukutu puppets (right)
These amusing dancing figures are attached by common bamboo arms.

First, thread string through the top of a card tube, then through a 15cm strip of bamboo, then a second card tube, then a second strip of bamboo, and tie off.

Make a nodding head from a sock end stuffed with paper and glued to the tops of the tubes, and add floppy legs with beads for the feet. Lastly, thread a long loop of string through the arms and over your toes. (It is easier with bare feet.) Slapping the thighs will make the figures dance about; or the hands could be free for a drum or a tambourine while the toes wiggle. Add bells, if you wish. The puppets could dance to a pop song or a nursery rhyme with a good beat, such as 'The Grand Old Duke of York'.

MAKING MUSIC TOGETHER

A waving puppet, such as the one in the photograph, can be used to 'conduct' class music.

He is made from a tin large enough to put a hand inside, with felt arms and clothes. Push a wooden control stick right through his hand and glue it in place. The top part is now his baton, and he can:

- conduct a group, or the class, using percussion instruments and taped music. The children must follow his signals, start and stop on cue, keep to the beat, play gently or vigorously.
- conduct a singing session, using the same signals. Practise 'internalising the beat': stop singing when the baton is still, but carry on singing the tune mentally until the baton starts again.
- conduct a session with singing and percussion, using a song such as:
  'I am a music man' (*Okki Tokki Unga*)
  'We can play on the big bass drum' (*Okki Tokki Unga*)
  'Playalong', (Eileen Diamond, *Rainbow Songbook*).
  Different percussion groups join in when they are mentioned in the song.
- Play 'Follow the action' game: the children copy the baton, and do precisely what it does - wave high or low, quickly, slowly, very slightly, in circles, tap on their heads, be still, etc.
- Tap out the rhythm of a favourite nursery rhyme, and see if the children can recognise it.
- Tap out a rhythm, which the children copy by clapping or tapping.

A holding puppet (see pages 19, 25 or 29) can pick up a beater or tambourine. Now it can:

- Play along to songs and taped music.
- Play 'Follow the action' game with sound effects.
- Play 'What can you hear behind the screen'. The puppet demonstrates five different shakers, then conceals them behind a screen. The children sing the song to the tune of 'Here we go round the Mulberry Bush', then listen to and identify the instrument the puppet is shaking.

A picking-up puppet could hold up signs, to show the children what to do:

- Traffic Lights: a red or green card 'lollipop' tells when to play or stop playing.
- Signs for groups of instruments (shakers, tappers, pluckers, scrapers, blowers) could be held up to show which instruments to play to the taped music.

43

LISTENING TO MUSIC WITH A STORY

'Peter and the Wolf', by Prokofiev

Peter (left)

For Peter, make a plastic head, as for the chef on page 23. Paste small pieces of newspaper smoothly over it, glue on paper feaures, and paint when dry.

Make the body from a plastic salt container, taped securely at the neck. Attach card tubes to the body with string to make flexible arms, and glue on floppy cloth trousers and wooden feet.

The puppet in the photograph has three strings, but it could have five, by adding strings to the knees to give leg control.

The Wolf (below)

The wolf's body is a washing-up liquid container covered with grey fur. For the floppy legs, make large holes in the bases of four little plastic containers, thread through string, and tie securely under the body. The head is black plastic foam, with a fixed, glued, lower jaw, and an upper jaw pivoted with a split pin, so the wolf will growl and snap when the string is pulled.

(NOTE: Weighting the snout with a metal bolt will make the jaw move more easily.)

Music with a good storyline lends itself well to dramatising with puppets.

Other musical stories to try:

'The Sorcerer's Apprentice' by Dukas;
'The Firebird' by Stravinsky;
'Hansel and Gretel' by Humperdinck.

SOUND EFFECTS

Children may wish to add sound effects to their performance of stories.

For instance, a dog may be waiting for the postman, and he hears:
- the gate open and shut
- footsteps coming up the path
- a knock at the door
- the letterbox opening
- the letters dropping in.

Then the dog barks and frightens him away.

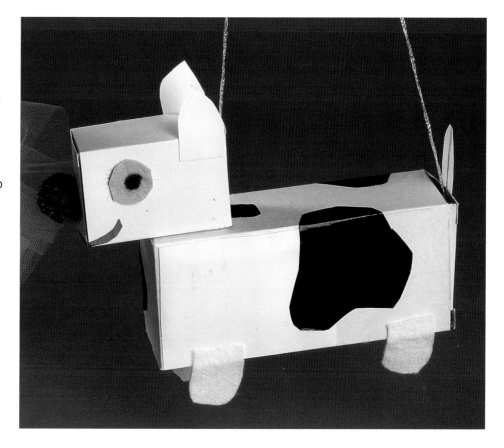

Spot, the dog, is made from two boxes turned inside out and glued together. Add a loop of string for easy control. All kinds of everyday items can be utilised to provide sound effects:

- horses' hooves with coconut shells or yoghurt pots knocked on a table
- fire, with crumpled Cellophane
- thunder, with a large piece of card shaken about
- rain, with rice on a tray (or a rainstick)
- birds singing, by rubbing a wet cork over the side of a glass bottle.

Percussion instruments have a huge range of 'voices' that can enhance a performance: from the dramatic clashing of cymbals, to the gentle tinkling of wind chimes; from the popping of temple blocks, to the deep, vague rumble or terrifying thud of a bass drum. The children will need to choose the instruments necessary to suit the action. They may need to make up some sound effects for:

- some spiky, icy, darting, tinkly music for Jack Frost
- a storm scene, with the rumble, crash, howl and splash of rain, wind and sea
- a conversation between monsters, with growling, snarling and snapping
- robot music, with motors, wheels and levers as the robot moves about
- a pirate story, sailing to a treasure island, searching and digging for treasure. (See *Three Singing Pigs* for a marvellous story on this theme, and for excellent ideas on adding sounds to a range of stories.)

Another way to add sound to a puppet story is to add a short musical excerpt at crucial points. For instance:

- In *The Musicians of Bremen* by Vera Southgate (Ladybird), when the animals set off on the road to Bremen, you could play Grofe's 'On the Trail' from 'The Grand Canyon Suite'.
- In *Patrick* by Quentin Blake (Cape) when Patrick leads a musical procession to town, you could play triumphal music such as Elgar's 'Pomp and Circumstance'.

Be alert for opportunities for listening to short excerpts of music to set the mood.

MUSIC TO FIT THE MOOD

Listening to music helps children to understand that communication reaches beyond the spoken word.

Interpreting the music with a puppet moving, dancing or acting, presents a non-threatening situation for the development of listening skills.

Pieces should be kept short, so that the children will want to hear more, and they should be encouraged to talk about the mood, so that they become active listeners.

GENTLE
- 'Dance of the Sugar Plum Fairy' ('Nutcracker Suite', Tchaikovsky)
  (**See ballerina above** - made with a paper cup)
- 'Moonlight Sonata' (Beethoven)
- 'Lullaby' (Brahms)

SCARY
- 'Trust in Me' (from 'The Jungle Book')
- 'Mars' (Holst - 'The Planets')
- 'In the Hall of the Mountain King (Grieg - 'Peer Gynt')

ANIMALS
- Carnival of the Animals' (Saint Säens)
- 'Les Anes' by Ingelbrecht (suggests donkeys baying, trotting, eating)
- 'The Ugly Duckling', sung by Danny Kaye

TOYS
- 'Toy Symphony' - 1st/2nd movt. (Haydn)
- 'Nutcracker Suite' (Tchaikovsky)
- 'The Fantastic Toy Show' (Rossini)
- 'Coppelia' (Delibes)

PROCESSIONAL
- 'Arrival of the Queen of Sheba' (Handel)
- 'Crown Imperial' (Walton)

SEA THEMES
- 'Noye's Fludde' (Britten)
- 'Sea Interludes' (Britten - 'Peter Grimes')

ELECTRONIC
- 'Sound Effects', BBC Record No. 1
- 'The Typewriter' and 'Syncopated Clock' (Leroy Anderson)

DANCE
- 'Norwegian Dance No 2' (Grieg)
- 'Rodeo' (Copland) - barn dances and square dances
- 'La Fille mal Gardee' (Herold - ribbon dance, clog dance, cock and hen dance)

LIVELY
- 'The Wasps' (Vaughan Williams)
- 'Flight of the Bumblebee' (Rimsky Korsakov)
- 'Eine Kleine Nacht Music' (Mozart)

CELEBRATORY
- 'Hallelujah Chorus' (Handel)
- 'Pomp and Circumstance' (Elgar)

MARCHING/BATTLE
- 'Aida' - Act 2, Scene 2 (Verdi)
- 'Occasional Oratorio' (Handel - 'March')

STORIES
FINGER PUPPET IN A STORY-BOOK

Prepare the books for the children by folding and stapling together two or three sheets of thin A4 card. Then cut a round hole right through the book from front to back. Sew a felt finger puppet, about 8cmx4cm, leaving the bottom 1.5cm of the side seams unstitched.

Decorate the puppet to make the animal or character of your choice, and then firmly glue the bottom edges around the back of the hole on the back cover so the puppet sticks out at the front.

The book is now ready for a story, and the puppet appears on every page in the story as it unfolds. These books are immensely popular with young children, and they will become engrossed playing with them, and telling the story to themselves and their friends, over and over again. The format of the book can be adapted to all kinds of classroom themes. It is particularly useful for repetitive stories, which are easily written and read by the children.

Some story ideas to try:
- A caterpillar eats a plum, apple, pear, etc., and turns into a butterfly.
- A puppy looks in various parts of the house for his bone.
- A rabbit eats his way through all the vegetables in the garden.
- A snowman (or Father Christmas) tells about his favourite Christmas things.
- An owl goes out and meets lots of nocturnal animals.
- A pirate digs in different places (jungle, swamp, beach, etc.) for treasure.

POCKET PUPPET IN A STORY-BOOK

A pocket of card can hold a little removable puppet from a familiar story such as 'The Gingerbread Man' **(see photograph)**. Make sure the pocket is not too tight at the top so the puppet can slip in and out.

Draw the puppet on paper with fabric crayons, then iron on to poly cotton, cut it out and glue it to a piece of biscuit-coloured felt, with a little padding under the body section.

Alternatively, a traditional finger puppet could go in the pocket.

Others to try:

- Baby Bear, from 'The Three Bears'
- The Troll, from 'The Three Billy Goats Gruff'
- Jack, from 'Jack in the Beanstalk'
- Cinderella.

Write your own story, from the puppet's point of view.

A shaped pocket book is always popular with young children.

The kangaroo book is made from two sheets of thin brown card folded and stapled along the spine.

Draw and cut out the kangaroo outline, and glue a card pocket to the front, ensuring that the top bows out well.

Stitch a little joey from oddments of felt, and lightly pad it. Attach him to the pocket so that he doesn't get lost.

Write a story about where he goes jumping, and what he meets on the way.

Other shaped pocket books to try:

- a basket outline, with a kitten in it
- a nest outline, with a chick in it
- a pram outline, with a baby in it
- a bed outline, with a child in it.

48

FINGER PUPPET STORIES

Comfortable tales with which the children are familiar can be performed by a child to himself/herself or to a small group.

A collection of short taped stories can be built up. If these are clearly labelled, the children can choose the story they want, and play out the action. Repetitive stories are thoroughly enjoyed by children, and help to develop early predicting skills, vital in learning to read.

Goldilocks and the Three Bears (left)

The Little Red Hen (above)

Performing to an audience is valuable socially. It encourages the children to see the value of taking turns, co-operating, and discussing ideas.

Role play can also be used to reinforce desirable behaviour.

Stories such as these show the importance of good manners, of helping a friend, and of non-aggression.

The Three Billy Goats Gruff (left)

49

TRADITIONAL FAIRY TALES

These amusing marionettes have clay heads, feet and heads, with a hole through each part to take the strings.

When the clay is dry, paint and decorate it to suit the chosen character.

To make the body, lay two pieces of string across a stiff piece of card, as in the drawing. Glue a piece of fabric right over the strings and 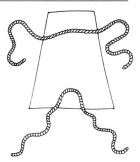 card, and trim off the excess. Glue the head firmly to the top of the body, overlapping at the top. Lastly, tie on the hands and feet, and attach three control strings.

These puppets are suitable for adapting to act out a wide range of fairy stories such as: *Hansel and Gretel, Little Red Riding Hood, The Nightingale, Jack and the Beanstalk, The Enormous Turnip, Cinderella, Aladdin, Snow White and the Seven Dwarfs, The Tinderbox*, etc.

Stories with plenty of action work well, and it is best to keep the dialogue short, so the narrative moves the drama along. A child may read the story, or tell it from memory. Younger children will need the teacher to narrate, or a short taped story.

Simple sound effects can be added at crucial points in the story, such as:
- whenever the 'baddie' comes on stage
- whenever Aladdin rubs his lamp
- whenever the Nightingale sings.

Older children may want to involve the audience: the puppet may ask their advice -
'Do you think I should ...?'; or it may ask 'Have you seen that dreadful wolf/giant/ sister, about today?'

MODERN TALES

The Hungry Caterpillar, by Eric Carle (Picture Puffin), is an extremely popular modern children's story, and can easily be adapted to puppetry.

To make the caterpillar, draw round an oval template twelve times, on wallpaper or printed card, red for the head and green for the body. Glue the ovals together in overlapping groups of three, then join each group together with a split pin, so the caterpillar will move freely at the joints. Tape sticks to the back of the first and third sections, and glue on other details. The food he eats could be drawn on cards taped to sticks, and you will also need a cocoon and a butterfly puppet to complete the story.

There is a delightful action song that complements this story - 'There's a tiny caterpillar on a leaf' (*Bobbie Shaftoe*).

There is an enormous range of excellent modern stories to choose from, if you wish to dramatise with puppets. Look for stories with strong characters and an easy-to-remember sequence of action. Some examples are:

- *The Jolly Postman*, by J&A Ahlberg (Heinemann)
- *Frog and Toad:* 'The Garden', by A. Lobel (Scholastic Inc.) - this has music and song too.
- 'Meg and Mog' stories, by Helen Nicoll (Picture Puffins)
- *Dear Zoo*, by R. Campbell (Picture Puffin)
- *One-eyed Jake*, by Pat Hutchins (Picture Puffin)
- *Not now Bernard*, by David McKee (Oliver and Boyd)
- *Burglar Bill*, by J&A Ahlberg (Heinemann)
- *Where the Wild Things are*, by Maurice Sendak (Harper & Row).

The stories may be taped or read exactly as they are. Alternatively, the children may keep the format but change the characters or the action slightly. They may invent a completely different ending of their own, or substitute a child in the class for the main character in the story. They may take the bare bones of the story and develop their own action, for example, by taking *But Martin* by June Counsel (Picture Corgi) and writing their own story of a visiting alien.

THE PUNCH AND JUDY TRADITION

Mr. Punch is a very old puppet, traceable back to the 16th Century Italian comic traditions, when the characters used witty dialogue, jokes and knockabout fun.

The English Mr Punch has been hitting puppets on the head for centuries - he does just what he likes and gets away with it!

(Watch a real Punch and Judy show for the best ideas.)

The Punch and Judy puppets above have papier mâché heads. To make these, soak thin newspaper strips in a bucket with water and powder paste to make a thick soup-like mixture. Mash thoroughly and drain very well.

Mould handfuls of stiff papier mâché round the top part of a strong card tube, keeping the lower part clear of paper (to form the neck). Make 3D features as exaggerated as possible, and smooth the surface well with a gluey finger. When the heads are thoroughly dry (slow baking in an oven will speed up the process), paint and decorate.

The body is made from two pieces of felt or cloth stitched around the edges, and glued firmly to the neck. Mr Punch traditionally has legs so that he can sit with his legs over the front of the stage. Wooden beads for feet will make a good thumping noise when he dances.
The baby is a strip of cloth rolled over a tube of newspaper. It could be a little cone shape so that it will stand up.

Mr Punch's movements are rapid and decisive. He can hold, throw, strike, and nod his head. His personality shows an honest admission of every human failing. A performance will include some or all of these traditional characters: Judy and the baby; Toby the dog; the policeman/officer; the doctor; Hector the horse; Jack Ketch the hangman; a crocodile, skeleton or devil. Punch is on stage nearly all the time, while the other characters come on one by one.

A performance will be a succession of incidents rather than a developing plot. Curtains are useful to raise the curiosity of the audience. You may add some music, and will need some props such as a stick, or a bell. Punch may deliberately throw his props off-stage (he throws other characters off-stage too!) so the audience has to hand them back.

☙ THE DRAMA OF MR PUNCH ☙

ENTER PUNCH:	He bows centre, right, left, and introduces himself. He dances and sings a song, sitting on the playboard. He beats time, crosses and uncrosses his legs to the music.
ENTER TOBY THE DOG:	Punch tells him, nervously, he's a good dog. Toby barks, snarls, bites him on the nose. Toby chases Punch (holding his nose) around.　　(EXIT BOTH)
ENTER PUNCH:	Asks the audience if the fierce dog has gone.
ENTER JUDY WITH BABY:	Punch wants a kiss, but she won't give him one. Judy tells Punch he's got to mind the baby. He gives it back, but she insists.　　(EXIT JUDY) Punch doesn't know what to do - the baby cries. Punch sings it a song - the baby cries louder. He waves it about crossly, and throws it off-stage.
ENTER JUDY:	She asks the audience where the baby is. Judy cries for the poor little baby, then gets a stick. She hits Punch with the stick - they fight. Punch throws Judy off-stage. He calls for his horse.
ENTER HECTOR THE HORSE:	Mr Punch asks him for a ride, but Hector won't be still. Punch gets on, and Hector throws him off backwards. Punch gets on, and Hector throws him off forwards. Hector gallops off-stage. Punch staggers about. Punch says his bones are broken, and calls for the doctor.
ENTER DOCTOR:	The doctor examines Punch, and Punch kicks him. The doctor hits him a few times to make him better! Punch hits the doctor with his stick, throws him off-stage. Punch gets his bell and runs about, making a noise.
ENTER POLICEMAN:	Tells Punch to be quiet. Punch stops, then carries on ringing his bell. Policeman says he's come to arrest Punch for three murders. They wrestle, and Punch runs away.　　(EXIT BOTH)
ENTER PUNCH (with sausages):	Asks audience if they like his sausages. Says he is feeling hungry - will have them for lunch.
ENTER CROCODILE:	Crocodile snaps at Punch - he jumps about the stage. Crocodile wants his sausages. Punch says 'Open wide'. Punch puts a stick (instead of sausages) into the crocodile's mouth. 　　(EXIT CROCODILE WITH MOUTH PROPPED OPEN)
ENTER DEVIL:	Brandishes a stick and tells Punch he's been very wicked. He chases Punch around and there is a fierce combat. Punch wins and the devil falls back. Mr Punch says he knows he's been a naughty boy. Then he brightens up, sits on the playboard and sings.

TALES WITH A MORAL

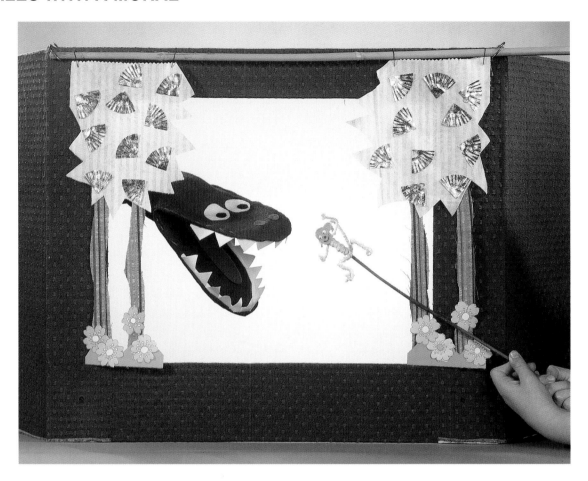

Puppets are a compelling vehicle for delivering moral messages: the 'goodie' always wins and the 'baddie' gets his come-uppance, as in *The Enormous Crocodile* by Roald Dahl (Puffin). The audience will love joining in with 'boos' and 'hurrahs'.

The crocodile. To make the sleeve puppet (crocodile), shown in the photograph above, you will need three pieces of green felt, cut as in the drawing, about 36cm x 11cm.

Cut a piece of stiff card, slightly smaller than the mouth section, and glue it centrally. Fold the mouth in half, card out, and glue the body sections to the upper and lower jaw (glue only half way along the card). Stitch together the sides of the mouth and the side seams and add felt details and card teeth. The crocodile makes wonderful snapping movements and sounds.

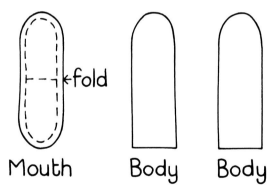

The monkey. Mugglewump, the monkey, is made from twisted pipecleaners and a felt head on a stick. (For details of the theatre, see page 68.)

Aesop's fables are an excellent source for moral messages, acted by puppets:
- 'The Honest Woodcutter' - honesty is the best policy
- 'The Sun and the Wind' - warmth and gentleness are stronger than bullying and boastfulness
- 'The Boy who cried Wolf' - always tell the truth
- 'The Musicians of Bremen' - friends should stick together...and many more.

There are a large number of modern stories that also contain moral messages, such as:
- *Tiddalik, the frog who caused a flood*, by R. Roennfeldt (Puffin) - sharing limited resources.
- *Tusk Tusk*, by David McKee (Anderson Press) - the colour of skin should not cause quarrels.

THE CHRISTMAS STORY

A Christmas tableau made from puppets will generate considerable interest as the children re-tell the story of the birth of Jesus. A tableau is a charming Christmas decoration set up in a corner of the school, and may be kept for several years. All types of stand-up figures may be made: the bodies could be a bottle, a cone, a box or a paper cup.

The slide-on puppets shown here are made from triangles of stiff card, folded centrally so they will stand up. Add a card circle for the head, and decorate lavishly with fabrics, glitter, etc. Tape each figure firmly to the end of a long strip of very stiff card, so they can slide on and off as the story is told.

The stable is made from a large box with openings cut at the front and side. Cover roughly with sacking, and shine a spotlight on your tableau.

THE MAHABHARATA

The epic poems 'The Mahabharata' and 'The Ramayana' are immensely popular in traditional Indian puppetry performances. Serious performances show the victory of Good over Evil and can take several weeks to complete a cycle of plays. The story below is one of the episodes from the Mahabharata.

NALA AND DAMAYANTI

King Nala, a handsome, gifted horseman, was in love with the most beautiful Princess Damayanti, and she with him. They had heard many praises of each other, but had never met. The Princess's father, King Bhima, decided to hold a husband-choosing ceremony, a svayamvara, for her. Nala, along with many other kings, resolved to go and win her hand.

On the journey to King Bhima's lands, Nala met with four of the Immortals: Indra, chief of the Gods; Agni, God of Fire; Varuna, God of Water; and Yama, Lord of the Underworld. They commanded him to deliver a message to the Princess - she was to choose one of the Gods for her husband. Nala soon met Damayanti, their love blossomed, and she swore she would not marry any God, but only Nala would be her Lord.

At the svayamvara, the four Gods changed their form to that of Nala's, and Damayanti was filled with such sadness when she could not choose the real Nala that the Gods were moved to pity. They helped her to see Nala's shadow and earthly form, and amidst great rejoicing, she chose and married Nala. The Gods bestowed great gifts on Nala - power over fire and water, and great skills in food preparation and journeying.

Now, the demon Kali wanted Damayanti to be his wife, and haunted the palace, trying to gain entry to Nala's heart. One day, Nala was playing a dice game with his brother, when the demon possessed him, and he gambled away all his treasures and his kingdom. Damayanti refused to leave her husband's side, though they now had nothing, but while she slept, Nala sped away, possessed by Kali. Damayanti searched the forests and towns for many weeks, but could not find him. She came to the city of Sabahu, where she was befriended by the Sabahu family, who took her in and sent messengers out to look for news of her husband.

Nala, wandering in the forest, came upon Karkotaka, King of Serpents, imprisoned in a huge fire and calling for help. Nala put his hands into the fire and rescued him, with no harm to himself, and the grateful serpent helped Nala. First, he gave Nala a magic bite, which put pain and torment into the demons in Nala's body. Then, he changed Nala's kingly form to a short and twisted one, and told him to go in this disguise to the city of Rituparna, to work as a charioteer. Lastly, the Serpent gave Nala a magic garment, with which he could retain his true form.

Nala followed the serpent's advice, and was engaged as chief of horses to Rituparna. Rituparna admired the great skill of his charioteer at taming horses, and Nala (disguised as Vahuka the charioteer) admired the great skill of his master at the science of numbers. Each agreed to impart their skill to the other, and as soon as the skill of dice passed into Nala, the demon Kali flew out from his body, where he had been in great pain, and departed.

A messenger came to Damayanti, with the news of a short-armed, crooked charioteer, amazingly skilled with horses, who might be Nala. The princess broadcast the news that she was going to have a second svayamvara, hoping that Nala would come. Rituparna decided to go to the svayamvara, hoping for a wife, and was driven by his charioteer. When they arrived at the kingdom of King Bhima, Damayanti gave orders for Vahuka to be secretly watched while he was preparing his master's food. He could fill vessels with water by looking at them, and light a fire by holding up the kindling. She knew it must be Nala. He put on the serpent's magic garment, and assumed his own noble form, and they were reunited forever.

THE INDIAN STORY-TELLING TRADITION

India has a long tradition of puppetry as a performance art. Many traditional stories carry a moral message, and are extremely useful in school assemblies, as a means of introducing festivals, beliefs and folklore from people of other cultures.

Puppets add a touch of magic to the stories.

Performances of the epic poem 'The Ramayana' are held in Delhi at the Ram-lila festival. The story tells of how the handsome Prince Rama, favoured by the gods, was forced from his kingdom to live in the forest with Sita, and how, after many adventures with Ravana the demon king, and Hanuman the monkey, they returned to their own land.

(See *The Infant Assembly Book* for details of this story, and of Diwali, the Hindu Festival of Lights.)

To make the puppets above, push a piece of dowelling firmly into a ball of clay (for the head), shape the features, and paint the head when dry.

Cut out the clothes (see line drawing) from fabric, and decorate lavishly with printed patterns in gold, silver, red and glitter. Cut a small central cross in the fabric, push the stick through, and glue the clothes at the neck. The side seams may be glued or stitched. Add hands and feet.
(Make the puppets quite large if they are to be used for assemblies.)

Other popular tales from Indian mythology suitable for puppet dramatisation are:

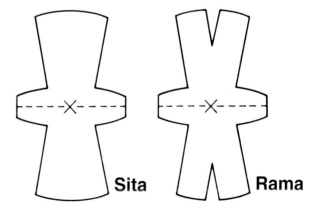

- The story of how the god Vishnu gave a woman a powerful protective thread to tie round her husband to protect him from an evil demon. (See *The Infant Assembly Book.*) This is the source of the Hindu festival of Raksha Bandhan, meaning 'ties of protection', when sisters honour their brothers by tying a band of threads called a rhaki around their wrists.

- The story of how Durga, the female champion of the gods, defeats the evil buffalo demon, and how all the gods helped her in her victory. (See *The Infant Assembly Book.*) This is the source of the festival of Durga Puja.

STORIES FROM CHINA

Dragon stories are particularly popular in Chinese mythology, in contrast to European stories (such as St George and the Dragon), where dragons are more feared than admired.

Four dragons were believed to rule over the four seas that surrounded the earth, and dragon kings could also be found in lakes and rivers, in crystal palaces filled with precious treasure.

The Dragon Dance is part of the New Year celebrations, where the dragon dances through the streets opening and closing its mouth and collecting gifts of money in lucky red envelopes. It is constructed so that people can move and dance inside it, and it therefore has affinities with the English Morris dancers' Hobby Hoss or the Caribbean Carnival characters, or the Big Bird puppet from 'Sesame Street', in that the puppeteer is actually inside the body of the puppet itself.

A dragon can be made quite easily for children's use by making a brightly decorated head from a cardboard box with a line of children behind it, each supporting a section of the dragon's body (a colourful blanket or piece of fabric, or garden netting).

Some popular Chinese stories to dramatise for puppet use could be:

- The Willow Pattern story is the famous love story of how a boy and girl were parted and reunited (see *The Willow Pattern Story* by Lucienne Fontannaz, Angus & Robertson).
- Stories about Monkey, his mischievous antics, and skill at martial arts, are greatly enjoyed by Chinese audiences (see 'The Monkey who would be King' from *Myths and Legends.*
- 'The Monster and the Red Doors' (see *The Infant Assembly Book*) tells the tale of why it is good luck to put red paper on the door in the Chinese New Year.
- The story of 'Nien the Monster' (see *The Tinderbox Assembly Book*).
- The ever-popular story of how the animals named the years is excellent for puppet dramatisation, showing how the twelve animals crossed the river (see *The Tinderbox Assembly Book*).
- The story of 'How the Cock got his Comb' (see *Myths and Legends from Around the World*).

AROUND-THE-WORLD STORIES FOR PUPPETS

The oral story-telling tradition is very strong in many countries in the world, and music, puppets or dance may be used to tell the story, which may be embellished or simplified, depending on the audience. Some story themes occur again and again all over the world, as people seek to explain how their world came to be - cleverness outwits force, and people and animals continue to do brave, foolish or wicked things.

Greek Myths

Many of the traditional stories are very exciting, with lots of action involving monsters, witches, gods and goddesses - excellent for puppetry. Marcia William's *Greek Myths for Young Children* (Walker Books) has a very funny strip cartoon format, with speech bubble dialogue instantly adaptable for puppet drama. Try particularly:

- Orpheus and Eurydice: opportunities for music, ghosts, monsters, hero rescuing heroine

- The Twelve Tasks of Heracles: exciting action with monsters and wild animals

- Perseus and the Gorgon's Head: traditional hero versus monsters.

African American

Uncle Remus' stories of Brer Rabbit's tricks and escapades are collected from centuries of oral transmissions. The story themes, as told by Joel Chandler Harris, are universal - the triumph of the little man over stronger and less cunning enemies. For puppet drama, try:

- *The Wonderful Tar Baby*

- *Brer Rabbit is Billy Malone*, stories from Joel Chandler's selection (Pelham Books).

African Folk Tales

- 'The Awongalema Tree' (from *Three Singing Pigs*) is a Zambian tale of how all the animals try to avert famine, and how only the slow little tortoise succeeds at the task.

- *Bringing the Rain to Kapiti Plain*, by V. Aardema (Picture Mac) is lovely for shadow or stick puppet performances.

- *How Stories Came into the World*, by Joanna Troughton (Blackie), includes Nigerian traditional stories such as 'Why Sun and Moon live in the sky', or 'How animals came to the earth'.

- 'Clever Rabbit and King Lion' by Amoafi Kwapong, from *Time for Telling*, is a story from Ghana of how a little animal outwitted the King of the Forest.

- *African Myths and Legends*, by Kathleen Arnott (Oxford University Press) has an excellent assortment of stories for dramatising, such as 'The Snake Chief' and 'The Tale of Superman'.

Scandinavian Stories

- *East o' the Sun and West o' the Moon*, by Walker Books, is an old Norwegian tale, and perfect story-telling: a magic spell that must be broken, and a fearless girl who journeys through all dangers to achieve her heart's desire.

- 'The Stolen Hammer of Thor' (see *Myths and Legends* by Anthony Horowitz) is one of the traditional Norse myths, which could be well adapted for use with puppets.

Caribbean Tales

The Caribbean has a living tradition of Carnival rather than a historical tradition of puppets, but many of its songs, stories and carnival characters could easily be used in a puppet performance:

- The Jamaican song, 'Linsted Market' (see *Ta-ra-ra boom-de-ay*) could have puppet buyers and traders in a colourful market scene, selling their wares of fish, yams, ackees, etc.

- Many of the tales of Anancy, the lazy boastful spiderman, are terrific for puppets, telling of how he tricks his way out of trouble, or into a worse mess! *Caribbean Stories*, by Robert Hull (Wayland) includes several Anancy tales, such as how he tried to get married.

- The Dominican story of 'Kakarat' (from *Tales, Myths and Legends*) is another traditional one of how a sensible boy outwits a monster.

PUTTING ON A PERFORMANCE

A PLAN OF CAMPAIGN

(See Page 2 for photograph relating to the example of performance given below)

WHAT TO DO	EXAMPLE
1. Choose a story outline with plenty of action. You may want to use a moral or safety message, such as: *Don't play with fire; Tell the truth; Don't throw litter,* etc. (Make sure something happens - someone is lost or rescued; someone is scared; finding treasure or a magic key, and so on.)	STORYSTART A 'funnybones' skeleton goes on holiday to Old McDonald's farm.
2. Make a list of the puppets that will be needed. They must be a suitable size and have the freedom of movement to do what is required. The characters need to be easily recognisable as good or bad, happy, sad, kind or selfish. Decide on the type of puppets you need (string, stick, etc.) and make them.	TYPE - Talking yoghurt pot heads, card bodies. CHARACTERS - skeleton, pig, cow, duck, horse, farmer.
3. Elaborate the storyline. Give it a PROBLEM that needs to be solved, an exciting CLIMAX, and a happy ENDING. Try out sections of the story, perhaps starting with the climax, allowing the children to improvise and develop their own ideas. Make a note of the best ideas, and add jottings on useful sections dialogue.	PROBLEM - The skeleton is friendly, but scares away all the animals. CLIMAX - The farmer is cross and chases the skeleton. ENDING - Explanations. Skeleton enjoys his holiday.
4. Decide whether the plot will be improvised or scripted. Dialogue needs to be kept short. Children's performances can be very successful without a written script, but it is important to list the scenes showing the story outline. Alternatively, a series of simple picture outlines can be drawn to show the sequence of action, and pinned up as an *aide-mémoire.* Written scripts may be learned by the puppeteers, read by a storyteller or put on to tape.	LIST SCENES AND IMPROVISE Skeleton meets each animal. Skeleton meets farmer. All animals sing. WRITTEN SCRIPT No.
5. Decide on props, scenery, lighting and sound.	PROPS - No. SOUND - Animal noises
6. Allow plenty of time to experiment with the puppets to develop their character and voices. Rehearse the play, gradually refining what has been improvised. Enjoy the performance. If performing to parents, you may wish to design programmes. Making a video of the performance gives an opportunity to enjoy it again, and look for areas of improvement next time.	MUSIC - Sing 'Old McDonald' at the end. LIGHTING - No.

STORYSTARTS

Storystarts with younger children

Get the children thinking about stories that they know, and encourage them to remember what happens and to become good listeners. You may show the children a Bookworm puppet who is sad because he has read all the books in the world. He asks the pupils what books they have read, and asks to be reminded what the book is about. He sadly says 'I've read that one. Can you tell me another?'

Pass around a puppet in circle time, and start off a story by saying, for example, 'Once there was a very greedy duckling'. The children each try to add one sentence to the story, which could be taped or made into a book, or dramatised in a performance with other puppets.

Simple REPETITIVE storylines work well with younger children:

- A child has lost its pet snake (ball, toy) and asks everyone he meets 'Have you seen my snake?' The snake can keep popping up and disappearing.
- A crocodile (bear, fox) is very hungry, and asks everyone 'Are you good to eat?'
- Mother hen is sitting on a clutch of eggs - what comes out of each one?
- A dragon (spider, giant) is lonely. Everyone is afraid of it, so he goes looking for a friend. (Read the poem 'The Lonely Dragon' by Theresa Heine, *Another First Poetry Book*.)
- A girl is sick in bed. Friends come knocking at the door to cheer her up. (e.g. Red Riding Hood, Baby Bear, a fairy godmother).
- A forgetful king can't remember where he put his crown, and everyone in the castle has to look for it (princess, queen, guard, cook, maid, etc.).
- A bird needs a place to build a nest. Its friends help it to find a perfect place.
- Joanna needs 'something special' for her mother's birthday present, and visits all the shops (greengrocer, baker, sweetshop, florist, etc.) until she finds what she wants.
- A duckling gets lost, and looks in various places (mouse's hole, hen's nest, dog kennel, beehive, fox's hole) until he finds his pond again.

Always try to think of something exciting (climax) and a happy ending.

Storystarts for older children

- A robber drinks a magic potion which makes him invisible, so he can steal...
- A princess cannot laugh - clowns and doctors try - but the only cure is to get some of the giant's magic laughing potion...
- A child is looking at a dinosaur skeleton in a museum, when it comes to life...
- Santa got stuck in the chimney - how did the reindeer get him out?
- A Chief Monster from the planet Cosmos visits the earth and captures a pet cat. How do the boy and girl rescue it?
- A fairy makes a magic dust which causes people to meow like cats - what happens?
- A man is bothered by dive-bombing creatures and swats them - what happened with the mosquito, fly, stag beetle, bat, eagle, pterodactyl?
- A gentle dragon is very clumsy - he breaks the furniture, trips over, eats huge meals. What happens when he laughs, sneezes, snores or deals with bullies?
- Sam has a new carpet in his room, but if he sits on it at night, it takes him to...(Dracula's castle, Treasure Island, the North Pole, Jurassic Park).
- Simon found a magic ring which made him shrink. He met a giant....(snail, bee, etc.)
- One house has a friendly dog, and one has a barking, snapping one. What happens to callers at the houses (milkman, paper girl, postman, window cleaner)?
- A diver is under the sea, finds treasure, but gets caught in a fishing net...
- A pirate ship hits a heavy storm, and the ship starts to sink...
- A toy robot gets bored with being still. He looks forward to night-time, when he can go whizzing round the shop floor and...

DEVELOPING THE PUPPET'S CHARACTER

The monsters are made by folding a paper plate in half, and gluing a card loop to the top and bottom of it, so the hand can open and close the mouth.

Make a slit in a carrier bag, and staple in the paper plate.

Glue on dramatic features (nothing too heavy, or the bag will not stand upright by itself).

It is important to allow plenty of time to find out what the character can do, and to develop its personality, so the audience will believe in it. Try it out in free play before a mirror, thinking about:

MOVEMENT - The puppet needs to move when it is talking, so the audience knows which character is speaking. Practise making it walk about, so it looks as though it has legs. Try to make it run, skip, sit down and go to sleep. Make it creep about and jump out to scare someone. Take it up and down stairs, make it pop in and out, or trip and fall over. Some puppets may be able to wave, point or scratch an itch. They may pick up or throw items to the audience, or nod and shake their head. Pretend your puppet is walking on ice, or has a broken leg. Two puppets may work together to pick up a treasure box, pull on a rope, or have a fight, and will need to face each other when having a conversation.

VOICE - Each character in a story needs to have a different voice. Try developing different voices by saying a simple sentence (for example, 'Has anybody seen my key, boys and girls?') in the voice of the character. Try thoughtful, grumpy, timid, mischievous, complaining, evil or happy voices. Try the voice of a snake, a robot, a mouse or a giant. Get your puppet to cry, laugh or scream, in character.

EMOTION - Try getting your puppet to show sadness, happiness, surprise, anger, fear, excitement, amusement or nervousness. Is it shy, confident or aggressive?

Typical characters in a story need to practise their own particular mannerisms. For example:

The villain needs to practise an evil walk and laugh, sneaking about, fighting the hero.

The hero/heroine needs to practise listening to cries for help, getting ready to fight, falling in love, fighting, rescuing the victim.

The monster needs to practise a scary voice and laugh, looking hungry or aggressive, ponderously walking, and leaping out to scare people.

PROPS AND ACTION TIPS

Puppets

If there is limited room in the performance area, it is best to have only two or three puppets on stage at a time. Make sure the puppets can be seen, and that they do not sink below the level of the stage. Keep the puppet as far to the front as you can, and tip it forward if the audience is at a lower level. Get the puppet to involve the audience now and then, such as by asking for their help with singing a song. Remember that taped stories provide little opportunity for involving the audience or for spontaneous improvisation.

Scenery

Scenery should be as simple as possible, and you may not need it at all. Complicated scenery changes will make the audience restless, and too much scenery can get in the way. Free-standing scenery may stay as a permanent part of the performance, making a useful place for the puppeteer to hide behind. Or it may be quickly slid on to the stage when needed.

The house, trees and sign (right) are cut-outs on stiff card with a box or block of wood glued behind so they stand upright. They may be painted in detail, or be simple sponge-printed outlines. You might try a castle outline, a boat, a bridge, a tower, a beehive, a rock with a cave in it, or whatever is needed for the action. A pair of wellingtons on stage next to a little puppet can give the idea of a giant.

Props

Props can be used to give an extra element of fun or surprise in a play or conversation, but be very wary of overdoing it, and only use props if they are necessary or add to the atmosphere or action. Have all props ready to hand for a performance, with props on sticks standing ready in a jar. Props may be introduced in a number of ways:

- They may be held by the puppet. The action may need a megaphone, a mirror, a magic wand, a frying pan or a telephone. A clown may have a balloon on a stick. A hanky may be needed for a puppet telling a sad story. An amusing idea is for the puppet to have a broken prop and try to sell it - a clock with no hands, a teapot with no spout, or a paintbrush with no bristles!

- Some props may need a string: clouds, sun and moon; an aeroplane or rocket; a snake coming out of a basket; chairs and tables dancing in a magic spell.

- Props may be on a stick and held up when needed, such as a ladder, a bed or a box of treasure. A magic shell may give wise answers to the puppet's problems.

- Bubbles may be blown on stage if, for example, clothes are washed, or every time a magic wand is used.

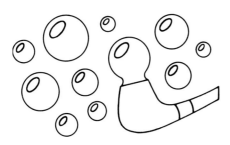

COSTUME

To make the reversible Indian male-female puppet above, start with a 40-45cm length of broomstick, and make a head for each end. Roll a thick tube of newspaper, and bend this into a curve for each head. Tape securely to the ends of the broomstick. Use papier mâché around each head shape to make a male and female face. Smooth carefully and, when dry, paint and add details. (This method of papier mâché for heads is much quicker to dry than that on page 52.)

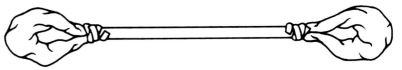

Glue a length of foam insulation tube around the stick, to give some padding to the bodies. Now add clothing, using glittery, silky or brightly coloured fabrics. Cut a circle of fabric for each figure, cut a cross in the centre for the neck, and tape securely around the neck from underneath. Put a little cotton wool padding on the chest, then bind a sash around the waists, glue on floppy arms or other decoration.

The puppet is quickly turned from male to female by inverting it, so one puppet could play two parts in a story, for example, a Princess and a Rajah. This type of puppet is useful if the play is about a person in disguise - a prince on one end, a pauper on the other. The costumes could be adapted for puppets from other countries, choosing suitable fabrics, hats, hair, and so on.

An idea to try in the classroom is to make a set of glove puppets with different hair and skin tones. Then give the children an assortment of pieces of fabric, robes, cloaks, hats, etc., and let them dress up the puppets as characters from different countries.

COSTUME

A basic hand puppet shape can be dressed in any type of regional costume you wish. You may be able to find a piece of fabric already printed in a suitable design, as in the African puppet, above. Alternatively, you can make your own design by patterning the fabric with felt-tip pens. The puppet heads are made from 7cm pieces of foam insulation tubing covered with the toe section of some tights (various colours can be used, depending on the skin tone required).

The children can make puppets to dramatise incidents from the past, to support topic work in History or Geography, **for example, the Egyptian stick puppets left**. These have Plasticine heads and card bodies decorated with fabric and glitter pens.

EASY THEATRES

Hand and Stick Puppets

In Rajasthan villages, the puppeteers are masters, but the theatre is a simple wooden frame with homespun cotton draped over it, lit by a hurricane lamp. The audience sits on the floor on straw mats.

A similar very easy theatre to make is a table-top one with a cloth over it to hide the puppeteers; or, a wall could be built around the table with large plastic bricks. Alternatively, a large piece of corrugated card could be put across the front, perhaps with an underwater scene, a night sky, or a Spring garden painted on it. The puppets appear above the table-top, and stand-up scenery can be put on the table. If there is a pinboard behind, a simple scene can be pinned to it for the backcloth. If the noticeboard is a free-standing type, then several scenes could be pinned to it, and quickly flipped over to the back when each one is needed.

A washing-line theatre is another simple way to hid the puppeteers. Tie a rope, just above head height, across the area to be used, and drape a piece of fabric over it. Look for possibilities in your classroom. You could use the window of the playhouse or class shop, or you could staple a piece of cloth across the lower half of a doorway. A piece of wood could be tied across two chair backs, draped with cloth, and card scenery could be stapled along the top.

A three-sided clothes-horse makes an excellent theatre **(see right).**

Tape paper to the two side sections, and drape a piece of fabric over the lower part of the middle section, leaving the centre open for the stage.

Tape a paper frieze along the top to finish it off.

String Puppets

The youngest children will not need a theatre for performing with string puppets. It is more instructive and more fun to start with a string, and attach an object to it such as a tennis ball, a bunch of keys or a handkerchief. The performer can then discover how to make the object bounce, jump, fly or climb on a chair. Try with elastic, too!

When the children are ready for a simple stage, the easiest one is made by placing a table on its side and either covering it with a piece of fabric, or taping a painted card strip around the three sides. The puppeteer stands behind, while the puppet walks on the floor in front. It may be rather difficult for the audience to see, unless they sit well back, so it is better to raise the table, if possible, by putting it on a step or a stage block. You may wish to tape silhouettes of trees, a town, or furniture in a room, to the cloth or card forming the backdrop.

The puppeteers, of course, will be seen. If you feel they need to be hidden, then hang a washing line above head height across the performance area, about 30-40cm in front of the overturned table. Hang a piece of fabric over this, so it just comes down to table height. If the cloth is the same colour as that used for covering the table, then the whole area may be treated as one large background, and may, for instance, be covered with stars and a moon on dark blue velvet, for a night-time scene.

THEATRES FOR TINY PUPPETS

Finger puppet play is often solitary, and a small child may be quite happy to tell himself a rhyme or story, or sing a song, using one or more puppets.

A small group of children may co-operate in telling a story together without the need for any props, scenery or theatre.

There may be occasions when a finger puppet theatre can add an extra element of fun to performing.

A little theatre (see above) can be made with a shoebox, stood on end, with a hole cut near the top. Paint and decorate it, and add curtains and a silky backcloth if you wish (glue this to the top of the box, at the back).

The little puppets (right) are cut-out photographs of the children, taken at school on "dressing-up day", and glued to lolly-sticks. The puppets shown are all book characters - a lost boy (Peter Pan), Rupert, Wally, and a dragon.

The easiest way to make a 'stage' is to drape a piece of fabric over a small box on a table, so the puppets appear above the 'stage' or box.
Finger puppets are small enough to look out of windows and doors cut from a stand-up card outline. Put folded sections at the sides to make it stable.

- A Noah's Ark outline could have animals and people looking out of holes and windows.

- **A castle outline** (see line drawing) could have royalty, servants, guards, ghosts, knights, and a dragon appearing at windows, towers and battlements.

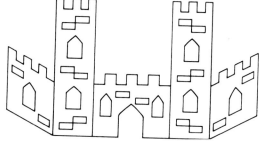

An interesting miniature theatre is in use in Japan, where a box is hung from the neck of the puppeteer, similar to the tray carried in a cinema by ice-cream sellers. The puppets are on sticks, slid on-stage through side openings cut in the box.

FOLDING TABLE-TOP THEATRES

Folding theatres may be made in all sizes. The little castle for finger-puppets on page 67 can be made large enough for hand puppets. A very large three-sided folding theatre may be cut from a giant cardboard carton, painted and decorated, and stood on the floor. Another folding type is the television screen shown on page 23.

The theatre shown above is a very versatile table-top type suitable for hand, stick and shadow puppets. On page 9, it is shown with a shadow screen clipped to the front. On page 54, it is shown with scenery hung from the bamboo at the top. This could be a tree, a tower, a house, or whatever, cut from card or fabric, with plenty of spaces for the puppets in between.

Above, the same theatre is shown with curtains hung from the bamboo, a decorative frieze taped to the top, and a playboard at the front for Mr Punch to sit on. To make the theatre, use three pieces of heavy-duty card, with an oblong cut from the central piece. Cover the whole thing with strong fabric, inside and out, so the fabric joins the three pieces of card together, making flexible side folds. (The theatre will then fold flat for storage.) Mr. Punch's playboard can simply be a row of wooden or plastic bricks, covered, if you wish, with fabric or paper. Cover the table with a large piece of cloth to hide the puppeteers.

You can be very imaginative with the shape of a three-sided table-top theatre, adapting it to suit the story. It could have any number of openings, with low sections where the puppets appear above, or holes cut out where the puppets look through. **It could incorporate a castle, a garden, and a dragon's cave (see drawing, right)** or a house, a shop or a seaside scene.

When you have finished playing, the theatre can simply be folded away.

Cut out the shaded sections.

BOX THEATRES

One of the easiest type of box theatres to make is the one photographed on page 55. Openings are cut in the front and the sides, and the stick puppets slide in and out through the sides. Alternatively, the top could be open instead of the sides, and the stick puppets then enter the stage from above. Small openings could then be cut in the sides for shining coloured torches through.

Both the examples below are of theatres which have scenery that can be changed, though you may wish to have just one fixed backdrop.

Side Entry Theatre
Cut out large openings at the sides and fold these forward to make curved 'wings'. The top of the box is open, with a pair of notches cut near the back, so the scenery will drop down into the notches. Attach sticks to the sides of the puppets.

Painted scenery glued to a dowel

Top Entry Theatre
Remove the top of the box, and cut notches to hold the scenery (as above).
Small windows have been cut in the sides for shining torches through. You could have several windows cut out, each covered with a different coloured Cellophane.
Attach the sticks to the top of the puppets.

If you want to add curtains, they could be hung on a piece of dowel pushed through the box above the front of the stage. Alternatively, thread string through the top hem of the curtains, and tie the string at the sides to split pins.

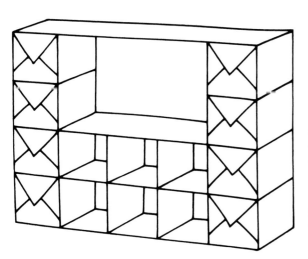

A permanent floor-standing theatre may be made by collecting 14 equal-sized medium cardboard boxes. Glue these together, so that there are four on each side and two rows of three in the middle.

Seal the flaps on the side boxes. Glue a piece of strong card across the stage area, and on top of the theatre, then wallpaper the whole structure. Paint or decorate as you wish.

From the back, the puppeteer has access to six useful compartments for storing props and puppets. At the front, curtains may be hung.

SHADOW PUPPETS AND OVERHEAD PROJECTORS

There are three essentials for shadow puppetry:

A SCREEN

The screen must be translucent, as is the one photographed on page 9. This is a piece of fine cotton muslin glued to a strong card frame, and temporarily attached to an all-purpose table-top theatre, using split pins at each corner. (This means the screen can easily be removed so that the theatre can be used for other types of puppets.) Pieces of scenery may be taped to the front of the screen if you wish, such as a moon, or a roof-top.

A screen could also be made from white cotton or architects' drafting paper fixed to an old picture frame, clamped firmly to a table.

If a slide projector is used for a light source, then the screen does not need to be translucent - you can use a standard projecting screen or any plain white wall.

A LIGHT SOURCE

This can be a few strong torches directed at the screen from behind, and slightly above the puppeteers.

Much more efficient is a 100W adjustable lamp fixed very securely in a position where the puppeteer will not touch it accidentally. Children need to be very aware of the safety aspects when working near a hot light bulb. Carefully adjust the beam of the lamp, so the shadows of the puppets can be seen, but not those of the puppeteer. Try a blue or a red light bulb for some eerie effects.

An alternative is to use a slide projector for the light source, or an overhead projector. A screen will not be needed for these: shadows of puppets can be directly projected on to a white wall.

THE SILHOUETTES

Outlines are put between the screen and the light source, to make shadows depicting the action. Try experimenting with materials such as fern fronds, cake doilies, strings of glass beads and coloured toffee papers to make some imaginative scenery.

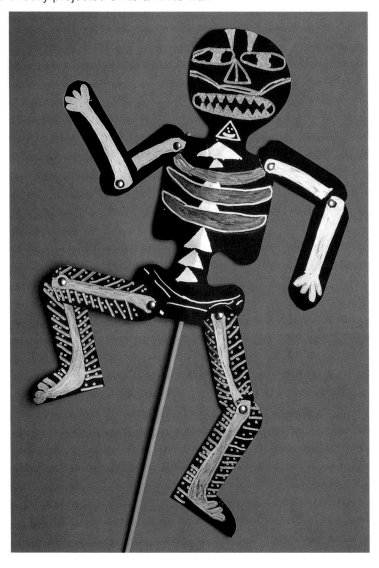

The puppets should not touch the screen. They may be articulated, or they may have cut-outs with coloured Cellophane behind.

Coloured shadow puppets can be made by cutting out the shape of the puppet on thin white card, and then colouring it on both sides with felt-tip pens or inks, so that the front and back match. Then rub both sides of the puppet with cooking oil to make it translucent - some of the colour will diffuse through the screen. Outline the figure with black for a good silhouette.

If an overhead projector is used to display the shadow puppets, then OHP pens and acetate film can be used for colourful effects. Try an underwater scene with mermaids, octopus, fish, a diver, and so on.

Try making a Bhoot Doll - or ghost doll - (see photograph right), an Indian toy with split pins to articulate all the joints. Attach it to a stick underneath. When the stick is rolled between the palms, the arms and legs fly about with amusing shadow effects.

RESOURCES

Rhymes and Poetry

This Little Puffin, compiled by E. Matterson.
The Mother Goose Treasury, R. Briggs (Puffin).
A Very First Poetry Book and *Another First Poetry Book*, John Foster (Oxford University Press).
The Puffin Book of 20th Century Children's Verse, Brian Patten, (Penguin Books).
The Oxford Book of Children's Verse, I. and P. Opie (Oxford University Press).
The Book of a Thousand Poems (Evans Bros. Ltd.).
Early Years Rhymes and Poems (Scholastic).
The Wandering Moon and other poems, James Reeve (Puffin).
Come Follow Me, Evans Brothers Ltd.

Music

A & C Black books
- *Okki-Tokki-Unga*
- *Tinderbox*
- *Apusskidu*
- *Game Songs*
- *Harlequin*
- *Birds and Beasts*
- *Bobbie Shaftoe*
- *Three Singing Pigs*
- *Ta-ra-ra boom-de-ay*
- *The Singing Sack*

The Music Box Songbook (BBC).
The Funny Family (Ward Lock Educational).
International Music Publications
- *Children's Funnyday Songbook*
- *Children's Sunnyday Songbook*
- *Eileen Diamond's Rainbow Songbook.*

Stories

The Infant Assembly Book, Doreen Vause (Macdonald Education)
The Tinderbox Assembly Book, Sylvia Barratt (A & C Black).
Tales, Myths and Legends (Scholastic Collections).
Seasons of Splendour, Madhur Jaffroy (Puffin).
Time for telling, Mary Medlicott (Kingfisher Books).
Myths and Legends, Anthony Horowitz (Kingfisher Books).
Aesop's Fables, Robert Mathias (Book Club Associates).

For details of further Belair publications
please write to:

BELAIR PUBLICATIONS LTD.
P.O. Box 12, TWICKENHAM, TW1 2QL, England

For sales and distribution (outside USA and Canada)
FOLENS PUBLISHERS
Albert House, Apex Business Centre
Boscombe Road, DUNSTABLE, Bedfordshire, LU5 4RL
England